U0084481

序 言

　　克漏字測驗向來是考生最頭痛的一大題，因為屬於綜合題型，出題方向包括文意、組織、文法概念等，考生不容易掌握要點。其實，只要考前多練習，熟悉考試重點，克漏字測驗並沒有想像中困難。

　　考試時，拿到題目不要緊張，先仔細觀察四個選項，若四個選項完全不相同，就是考句意，要注意上下文意；若四個選項大致相同，只是詞類或是時態不相同，便是考文法。會出現在克漏字測驗的文法，通常都不難，最常考的就是省略關代和 be 動詞的分詞片語，以及複合關代 what 和關係副詞 where、why 等。至於句意的部分，想要拿高分，就得要多背單字和片語。

　　「高二英文克漏字測驗」總共收錄了四十篇克漏字測驗，每一篇都是選自各校高二月期考試題，經由美籍老師仔細校訂，是最適合同學練習的題目。書中所有的文章都有翻譯及註釋，節省同學查字典的時間；並針對每一道題目仔細解說，對錯答案都有明確的交代。透過本書的練習，可以幫助你累積克漏字解題技巧及實力。

　　本書中的試題，全部經過「劉毅英文家教班」同學實際考過，效果甚佳。書後附有「本書答題錯誤率分析表」，切記，大家容易錯的地方，你一定要弄懂，因為那就是你勝過別人的關鍵。

　　本書編校製作過程嚴謹，但仍恐有疏失之處，祈盼各界先進不吝指正。

編者 謹識

TEST 1

Read the following passage and choose the best answer for each blank from the choices below.

From time to time most of us have to do some reading for some reason. We frequently deal with such an ___1___ with the idea of reading a certain number of pages, or starting at the beginning and reading page by page ___2___ we have completed the task. However, reading an article ___3___ through is by no means the most effective method of reading. We should preview the whole thing quickly to find out what is included and what the main points of the article ___4___. The better our initial understanding of our reading is, the ___5___ we can keep the information in mind and combine what we are reading and what we already know. 【陽明高中】

1. (A) examination   (B) assignment
   (C) example   (D) exploration

2. (A) until   (B) although
   (C) if   (D) when

3. (A) straightly   (B) straight
   (C) direct   (D) continual

4. (A) is   (B) has
   (C) have   (D) are

5. (A) more easily   (B) easier
   (C) more difficult   (D) harder

TEST 1 詳解

From time to time most of us have to do some reading for some reason. We frequently deal with such an <u>assignment</u> with
1

the idea of reading a certain number of pages, or starting at the beginning and reading page by page <u>until</u> we have completed the task.
2

我們大多數人時常必須因為某種理由而讀書。我們在閱讀時，常常會想要讀完幾頁，或是從開頭開始一頁一頁地讀，直到全部讀完。

** ***from time to time*** 時常　　reading〔'ridɪŋ〕*n.* 閱讀；讀書
for some reason 因為某種理由
frequently〔'frikwəntlɪ〕*adv.* 經常
deal with 處理　　***with the idea of*** 帶著…的念頭
certain〔'sɝtn̩〕*adj.* 某一；若干的
page by page 一頁接著一頁
complete〔kəm'plit〕*v.* 完成　　task〔tæsk〕*n.* 工作；任務

1. (**B**)　依句意，選 (B) ***assignment***〔ə'saɪnmənt〕*n.* 作業；任務。
而 (A) 考試，(C) 例子，(D) exploration〔ˌɛksplə'reʃən〕*n.*
探險，皆不合句意。

2. (**A**)　依句意，選 (A) ***until***「直到」。

However, reading an article <u>straight</u> through is by no means
3

the most effective method of reading. We should preview the whole thing quickly to find out what is included and what the main points of the article <u>are</u>.

4

然而，把文章從頭到尾讀完，絕對不是最有效的讀書方法。我們應該快速地把全部先看一遍，了解文章的內容，以及主旨為何。

    ** article〔'ɑrtɪkḷ〕*n.* 文章   ***by no means*** 絕不
         effective〔ɪ'fɛktɪv〕*adj.* 有效的   method〔'mɛθəd〕*n.* 方法
         preview〔'pri,vju〕*v.* 預看；預習   ***find out*** 查出；發現
         include〔ɪn'klud〕*v.* 包含   ***main point*** 主旨

3. (**B**) ***read ~ straight through*** 把 ~ 從頭到尾讀完
        空格應填副詞，且依句意，選 (B) ***straight***〔stret〕*adv.* 連
        續地；不斷地。(A) straightly〔'stretlɪ〕*adv.* 直直地，(C)
        direct〔də'rɛkt〕*adj.* 直接的，(D) continual〔kən'tɪnjʊəl〕
        adj. 持續不斷的，則用法與句意均不合。

4. (**D**) main points（主旨）為複數，故須用複數動詞，依句意，文
        章的主旨「是」什麼，選 (D) ***are***。

The better our initial understanding of our reading is, the
<u>more easily</u> we can keep the information in mind and combine
     5
what we are reading and what we already know.
我們對文章初步的了解越透徹，就越容易記住文章中的資料，並將所讀的內容與已知的知識相結合。

    ** initial〔ɪ'nɪʃəl〕*adj.* 最初的
         understanding〔,ʌndə'stændɪŋ〕*n.* 了解
         keep ~ in mind 記住 ~
         information〔,ɪnfə'meʃən〕*n.* 資訊；資料
         combine〔kəm'baɪn〕*v.* 結合

5. (**A**) 依句意，「更容易」記住資料，修飾動詞 keep 須用副詞，
        故選 (A) ***more easily***。而 (C) more difficult「更困難」，
        (D) harder「更困難；更努力」，均不合句意。

TEST 2

Read the following passage and choose the best answer for each blank from the choices below.

Attitude is everything. If you take knowledge, hard work and attitude and evaluate these ___1___, you'll find that attitude plays a far more important role in success than the other two. Take Jerry for example. He is a person who always holds a positive attitude ___2___ everything. He understands the power of choice, and chooses to look on the bright side of things.

___3___ his amazing attitude, he survived an armed robbery ___4___ he was held up at gunpoint and got shot. ___5___ he was wheeled to the emergency room with no hope of living out another day, he insisted on not being treated like a dead man. He has inspired lots of people to live their lives fully every day. 【景美女中】

1. (A) morals   (B) benefits
   (C) options   (D) factors

2. (A) in   (B) on
   (C) at   (D) toward

3. (A) Because   (B) As
   (C) Thanks to   (D) For

4. (A) in which   (B) which
   (C) that   (D) what

5. (A) Even when   (B) Whenever
   (C) If   (D) At the thought of

TEST 2 詳解

Attitude is everything. If you take knowledge, hard
work and attitude and evaluate these <u>factors</u>, you'll find
　　　　　　　　　　　　　　　　　　　　1
that attitude plays a far more important role in success than
the other two.

　　態度就是一切。如果你拿知識、努力和態度，並評估這些因素
，你會發現，態度跟其他兩者比起來，在成功上所扮演的角色重要
多了。

> ** attitude〔'ætə,tjud〕*n.* 態度
> ***hard work*** 努力
> evaluate〔ɪ'vælju,et〕*v.* 評估
> ***play an important role*** 扮演重要的角色

1. (**D**)　依句意，選 (D) ***factor***〔'fæktɚ〕*n.* 因素。而 (A) moral
　　　　〔'mɔrəl〕*n.* 寓意；敎訓，(B) benefit〔'bɛnəfɪt〕*n.* 利
　　　　益，(C) option〔'ɑpʃən〕*n.* 選擇，均不合句意。

Take Jerry for example. He is a person who always holds
a positive attitude <u>toward</u> everything. He understands the
　　　　　　　　　　　　　2
power of choice, and chooses to look on the bright side
of things.

以傑瑞爲例。他總是對任何事物都抱持樂觀的態度。他了解選擇
的力量，並選擇看事情的光明面。

** positive〔'pɑzətɪv〕*adj.* 積極的；樂觀的
hold a positive attitude 抱持樂觀的態度
choice〔tʃɔɪs〕*n.* 選擇　　choose〔tʃuz〕*v.* 選擇
look on the bright side of things 看事物的光明面

2. (**D**) attitude *to/toward* 對於～的態度

<u>Thanks to</u> his amazing attitude, he survived an armed
　　　　3
robbery <u>in which</u> he was held up at gunpoint and got shot.
　　　　　　 4
由於他這種令人驚奇的態度，在一場武裝搶劫案中，他被抓住而
被用槍指著，並且遭到槍擊，他還是生還。

** amazing〔ə'mezɪŋ〕*adj.* 令人驚奇的
survive〔sɚ'vaɪv〕*v.* 自～中生還
armed〔ɑrmd〕*adj.* 武裝的
robbery〔'rɑbərɪ〕*n.* 搶案　　***hold up*** 抓住
gunpoint〔'gʌn,pɔɪnt〕*n.* 槍口
at gunpoint 在槍口威脅下　　shoot〔ʃut〕*v.* 射擊

3. (**C**) 依句意，「由於」他令人驚奇的態度，故選 (C) ***Thanks
to***「由於；因為」。而 (A) Because「因為」為連接詞，
其後須接句子，在此不合；(B) As「身為」，(D) For
「為了」，則不合句意。

4. (**A**) 依句意，「在這場搶案當中」，選 (A) ***in which***。而 (B)
which，(C) that 為關係代名詞，做子句的主詞，其後
須接不完整句，在此用法不合；(D) what = the thing
that，用法與句意均不合。

Even when he was wheeled to the emergency room with
5
no hope of living out another day, he insisted on not being
treated like a dead man. He has inspired lots of people to
live their lives fully every day.

即使在他被送往急診室,而且幾乎連再活一天的希望都很渺茫時,
他還是堅持不要像個死人一樣被治療。傑瑞的態度激勵了很多人,
每天生活都要過得很充實。

> ** wheel〔hwil〕*v.* 用車子載運
> emergency〔ɪˈmɝdʒənsɪ〕*adj.* 緊急的
> ***emergency room*** 急診室　　***insist on*** 堅持
> treat〔trit〕*v.* 治療　　inspire〔ɪnˈspaɪr〕*v.* 激勵
> fully〔ˈfʊlɪ〕*adv.* 充分地

5. (**A**) 依句意,選 (A) ***Even when***「即使是當…的時候」。
　　　而 (B) whenever「無論何時」,(C) if「如果」,
　　　(D) at the thought of「一想到」,則不合句意。

┌─【劉毅老師的話】─────
│　　克漏字是同學最怕的部分,對於
│越怕的就越要練習。每做一回 Test 都
│是一項挑戰。
└────────────────

TEST 3

Read the following passage and choose the best answer for each blank from the choices below.

To have a high EQ ___1___ certain emotional skills. The first of these is self-awareness, ___2___ is the ability to recognize what we are feeling and how it is affecting us. Another basic EQ skill is self-control, or the ability to ___3___ our own emotions. If we meet with difficulties, we can look upon them as a challenge ___4___ giving up. A third skill of EQ is ___5___ "people skills," the ones that help us to get along well with other people. 【中正高中】

1. (A) acquires　　　　　　(B) inquires
   (C) requires　　　　　　(D) reconsiders

2. (A) that　　(B) which　　(C) how　　(D) it

3. (A) react　　(B) handle　　(C) respond　　(D) relate

4. (A) besides　　　　　　(B) in case of
   (C) instead of　　　　　(D) in spite of

5. (A) known as　　　　　(B) famous for
   (C) in favor of　　　　(D) done without

TEST 3 詳解

To have a high EQ <u>requires</u> certain emotional skills. The
                        1
first of these is self-awareness, <u>which</u> is the ability to recognize
                                        2
what we are feeling and how it is affecting us.

要擁有高情緒商數，需要某些處理情緒的技巧。首先就是要有自
我意識，也就是認清自己的感覺，以及這樣的感覺對我們有何影響。

** ***EQ*** 情緒商數（簡稱「情商」，表示自我情緒控制能力的指數）
    （ = *emotional quotient* ）【quotient〔'kwoʃənt〕*n.* 商數】
    certain〔'sɝtn̩〕*adj.* 某些；特定的
    emotional〔ɪ'moʃənl̩〕*adj.* 情緒的
    self-awareness〔'sɛlfə'wɛrnɪs〕*n.* 自我意識
    the ability to V. 做…的能力
    recognize〔'rɛkəg,naɪz〕*v.* 認清   affect〔ə'fɛkt〕*v.* 影響

1. (**C**) (A) acquire〔ə'kwaɪr〕*v.* 獲得
           (B) inquire〔ɪn'kwaɪr〕*v.* 詢問
           (C) ***require***〔rɪ'kwaɪr〕*v.* 需要
           (D) reconsider〔,rikən'sɪdɚ〕*v.* 再考慮

2. (**B**) 空格應填關代，引導形容詞子句，修飾先行詞
           self-awareness，又前有逗點，不可用 that，故選 (B)
           which。

Another basic EQ skill is self-control, or the ability to <u>handle</u>
                                                             3
our own emotions. If we meet with difficulties, we can look
upon them as a challenge <u>instead of</u> giving up.

另一個基本情緒商數技巧，就是自制，也就是控制自己情緒的能力。
如果我們遭遇困難，就要將它們視爲挑戰，而不要放棄。

>　** self-control 〔ˌsɛlfkənˈtrol〕 *n.* 自制
>　***meet with*** 遭遇　***look upon*** A ***as*** B　認爲 A 是 B
>　challenge 〔ˈtʃælɪndʒ〕 *n.* 挑戰　***give up*** 放棄

3.(**B**)　自制，也就是「處理」自己情緒的能力，選 (B) ***handle***
　　　　　〔ˈhændl̩〕 *v.* 應付；處理。而 (A) react 〔rɪˈækt〕 *v.* 反應，
　　　　　(C) respond 〔rɪˈspɑnd〕 *v.* 回答；回應，(D) relate 〔rɪˈlet〕
　　　　　v. 使有關連，則不合句意。

4.(**C**)　依句意，選 (C) ***instead of***「而不是」。而 (A) besides「除了
　　　　　…之外（還有）」，(B) in case of「如果發生」，(D) in
　　　　　spite of「儘管」，均不合句意。

A third skill of EQ is <u>known as</u> "people skills," the ones that
　　　　　　　　　　　　　5
help us to get along well with other people.
第三個情緒商數的技巧，被稱爲「人際關係處理技巧」，這技巧能幫
助我們與他人和諧相處。

>　** ***people skills*** 人際關係處理技巧
>　***get along well with*** 和…和諧相處

5.(**A**)　依句意，選 (A) ***be known as***「被稱爲」。而 (B) be famous
　　　　　for「以~聞名」，(C) in favor of「贊成」，(D) do without
　　　　　「免除；不用」，則不合句意。

TEST 4

Read the following passage and choose the best answer for each blank from the choices below.

Many years ago, just before the entrance examination, I accompanied my mother to a temple. ____1____ the temple, I was surrounded with solemnity. I heard my mother pray ____2____ the god ____2____ my good grades in the entrance examination. I still remember that whenever she prayed during those years, she would never forget to say, "Make my son strong enough to grow to be a man and smart enough to have good academic performance. Make him a man ____3____ well-shaped character and command of knowledge will lay the ____4____ of his future success." As time went on, I came to realize how dearly my mother loved me and what great expectations she had ____5____ me. 【松山高中】

1. (A) As soon as I entering

   (B) When entered

   (C) Upon entering

   (D) Hardly had he entered

2. (A) to ; for   (B) for ; for

   (C) for ; of   (D) X ; of

3. (A) that   (B) who

   (C) whose   (D) whom

4. (A) impact   (B) victory

   (C) backbone   (D) foundation

5. (A) by   (B) on

   (C) from   (D) of

TEST 4 詳解

Many years ago, just before the entrance examination, I accompanied my mother to a temple. <u>Upon entering</u> the temple,
                                                                          1
I was surrounded with solemnity. I heard my mother pray
<u>to</u> the god <u>for</u> my good grades in the entrance examination.
2   2

很多年前，就在入學考試之前，我陪我母親去一座廟。一進到廟裡，莊嚴的氣氛就包圍了我。我聽到母親向神明祈求，希望我在入學考試中能有好成績。

* ** entrance〔'ɛntrəns〕*n.* 進入；入學
* ***entrance examination*** 入學考試
* accompany〔ə'kʌmpənɪ〕*v.* 陪伴
* temple〔'tɛmpl̩〕*n.* 寺廟　　surround〔sə'raʊnd〕*v.* 環繞
* solemnity〔sə'lɛmnətɪ〕*n.* 嚴肅；莊嚴　　pray〔pre〕*v.* 祈禱

1. (**C**) 表「當我一進入寺廟」，可用：
   As soon as I ***entered*** the temple,⋯
   When ***I*** entered the temple,⋯
   Upon entering the temple,⋯
   Hardly had ***I*** entered the temple before⋯　　故選 (C)。

2. (**A**) pray ***to*** a god ***for*** ~　向神祈求~

I still remember that whenever she prayed during those years, she would never forget to say, "Make my son strong enough to grow to be a man and smart enough to have good academic performance. Make him a man <u>whose</u> well-shaped character
                                                    3
and command of knowledge will lay the <u>foundation</u> of his
                                                    4
future success."

我還記得在那幾年，每當她在祈求時，她絕不會忘記說：「讓我兒子夠
強壯能長大成人，夠聰明，能有好的學業成績。讓他成為一個有良好的
個性並且知識豐富的人，這能奠定他未來成功的基礎。」

＊＊ whenever〔hwɛn'ɛvɚ〕*conj.* 每當
　　 academic〔ˌækə'dɛmɪk〕*adj.* 學業的
　　 performance〔pɚ'fɔrməns〕*n.* 表現
　　 well-shaped〔'wɛl'ʃept〕*adj.* 形狀良好的；非常合適的
　　　【在此指「良好的」(= *good*)】
　　 character〔'kærɪktɚ〕*n.* 性格
　　 command〔kə'mænd〕*n.* 掌握；精通　　 lay〔le〕*v.* 奠定

3. (**C**) 空格應填關代的所有格，故選 (C) *whose*。

4. (**D**) 依句意，選 (D) *foundation*〔faʊn'deʃən〕*n.* 基礎。
　　　　 lay the foundation　奠定基礎
　　　　 而 (A) impact〔'ɪmpækt〕*n.* 影響，(B) victory〔'vɪktərɪ〕*n.*
　　　　 勝利，(C) backbone〔'bæk.bon〕*n.* 脊椎骨；骨氣，則不合
　　　　 句意。

As time went on, I came to realize how dearly my mother loved
me and what great expectations she had <u>of</u> me.
　　　　　　　　　　　　　　　　　　　　　5
隨著時間的過去，我才了解我母親有多麼愛我，以及她對我的期望有
多高。

＊＊ *as time goes on*　隨著時間的過去（ = *as time goes by* ）
　　 come to realize　了解　　 dearly〔'dɪrlɪ〕*adv.* 充滿深情地
　　 love sb. dearly　深愛某人
　　 expectation〔ˌɛkspɛk'teʃən〕*n.* 期望

5. (**D**) have great expectations *of sb.* 對某人期望很高

TEST 5

Read the following passage and choose the best answer for each blank from the choices below.

Ideas about friendship differ ___1___ person to person. For the French, it is a one-to-one relationship ___2___ requires knowledge of the individual's mind, character, and interests. A friend is someone who brings out the best in one. The French enjoy talking about intellectual topics, and arguments do not destroy friendship; ___3___, they are essential to developing friendship.

___4___ Germans, they form long-lasting friendships in their childhood, and friends become part of their family.

For Americans, friendship is less permanent because people move, change jobs, marry, or discover new interests. However, British friendships can

continue ___5___ after a long separation. One can

always take up one's friendship where one left off.

【成功高中】

1. (A) to (B) with
   (C) from (D) on

2. (A) who (B) that
   (C) whom (D) to

3. (A) however (B) nevertheless
   (C) but (D) instead

4. (A) In addition (B) As for
   (C) As a result (D) For

5. (A) even (B) than
   (C) with (D) like

TEST 5 詳解

Ideas about friendship differ <u>from</u> person to person. For
                                      1
the French, it is a one-to-one relationship <u>that</u> requires
                                               2
knowledge of the individual's mind, character, and interests.
A friend is someone who brings out the best in one. The
French enjoy talking about intellectual topics, and arguments
do not destroy friendship; <u>instead</u>, they are essential to
                              3
developing friendship.

　　每個人對友誼的想法都不同。對法國人來說，友誼是一對一的關
係，需要了解個人的心靈、性格，和興趣。朋友會激發自己最好的一
面。法國人喜歡談論知識性的話題，而這樣的爭論並不會破壞他們的
友誼；相反地，這對培養友誼而言是必要的。

　　** differ〔'dɪfɚ〕*v.* 不同　　***the French*** 法國人
　　　　one-to-one〔'wʌntə'wʌn〕*adj.* 一對一的
　　　　require〔rɪ'kwaɪr〕*v.* 需要
　　　　knowledge〔'nɑlɪdʒ〕*n.* 知識；熟知
　　　　individual〔ˌɪndə'vɪdʒuəl〕*n.* 個人
　　　　mind〔maɪnd〕*n.* 心靈　　character〔'kærɪktɚ〕*n.* 性格
　　　　bring out 發揮；引出
　　　　intellectual〔ˌɪntḷ'ɛktʃuəl〕*adj.* 知性的；智力的
　　　　argument〔'ɑrgjəmənt〕*n.* 爭論　　destroy〔dɪ'strɔɪ〕*v.* 破壞
　　　　essential〔ə'sɛnʃəl〕*adj.* 必要的　　develop〔dɪ'vɛləp〕*v.* 培養

1. (**C**) ***differ from person to person*** 每個人都不同

2. (**B**) that 引導形容詞子句，修飾先行詞 relationship。而 (A)
　　　　who 只能用於先行詞是人的情況，在此不合。

3. (**D**)　依句意，選 (D) *instead*「取而代之；相反地」。而 (A)
　　　　　 however「然而」，(B) nevertheless「然而；儘管如此」
　　　　　 (= *however*)，(C) but「但是」，均不合句意。

　　<u>As for</u> Germans, they form long-lasting friendships in their
　　　　　 4
childhood, and friends become part of their family.
　　至於德國人，他們在童年時期就建立持久的友誼，而且朋友會成
爲他們家庭的一份子。

　　** German〔'dʒɝmən〕*n.* 德國人　　form〔fɔrm〕*v.* 形成；建立
　　　　 long-lasting〔'lɔŋ'læstɪŋ〕*adj.* 持久的
　　　　 childhood〔'tʃaɪldˌhʊd〕*n.* 童年

4. (**B**)　依句意，選 (B) *As for*「至於」。而 (A) in addition「此外」，
　　　　　 (C) as a result「因此」，(D) for「對…而言；爲了」，則不
　　　　　 合句意。

　　For Americans, friendship is less permanent because people
move, change jobs, marry, or discover new interests. However,
British friendships can continue <u>even</u> after a long separation.
　　　　　　　　　　　　　　　　　　　　 5
One can always take up one's friendship where one left off.
　　對美國人而言，友誼較不長久，因爲人們會搬家、換工作、結
婚，或是發展新的興趣。然而，英國人即使在分開很長一段時間後，
友誼還是能持續。每個人都可以在友誼停滯的地方，繼續發展友誼。

　　** permanent〔'pɝmənənt〕*adj.* 永久的；持久的
　　　　 discover〔dɪ'skʌvɚ〕*v.* 發現；發掘
　　　　 British〔'brɪtɪʃ〕*adj.* 英國的　　continue〔kən'tɪnjʊ〕*v.* 持續
　　　　 separation〔ˌsɛpə'reʃən〕*n.* 分離
　　　　 take up 把…繼續下去；把…接下去　　*leave off* 停止

5. (**A**)　依句意，「即使」分開很長一段時間後，選 (A) *even*。

TEST 6

Read the following passage and choose the best answer for each blank from the choices below.

A good ad uses a catchy slogan or jingle, or an unusual image that will ___1___ easily by people. Almost everyone in America, for example, knows these famous words: "Things go better with Coke." The slogan is ___2___ an ad for a soft drink company. But a good slogan or image is just the first step in effective advertising. The people who ___3___ ads follow a set of four principles, which are known ___4___ AIDA. The "A" ___5___ attracting consumers' *attention*, the "I" and "D" are for arousing their *interest* and *desire*, and the final "A" is for encouraging them to take immediate *action*.

【中正高中】

1. (A) remember   (B) remembering
   (C) remembered   (D) be remembered

2. (A) to   (B) at
   (C) by   (D) from

3. (A) create   (B) created
   (C) creating   (D) are created

4. (A) as   (B) of
   (C) to   (D) for

5. (A) cares for   (B) looks for
   (C) stands for   (D) stands out

TEST 6 詳解

A good ad uses a catchy slogan or jingle, or an unusual image that will <u>be remembered</u> easily by people. Almost
$\quad\quad\quad$ 1
everyone in America, for example, knows these famous words: "Things go better with Coke." The slogan is <u>from</u> an ad for a
$\quad\quad\quad\quad\quad\quad\quad\quad\quad\quad\quad\quad$ 2
soft drink company.

一則好廣告會使用吸引人的標語或廣告歌，或與眾不同的形象，
容易讓人們記住。例如，幾乎每個美國人都聽過這句有名的話：「有
了可口可樂，食物更可口。」這個標語是來自於某個清涼飲料公司的
廣告。

** ad 〔 æd 〕 *n.* 廣告 (= *advertisement*)
catchy 〔'kætʃɪ 〕 *adj.* 引人注意的
slogan 〔'slogən 〕 *n.* 標語；口號　　jingle 〔'dʒɪŋgl 〕 *n.* 廣告歌曲
unusual 〔 ʌn'juʒʊəl 〕 *adj.* 不尋常的　　image 〔'ɪmɪdʒ 〕 *n.* 形象
Coke 〔 kok 〕 *n.* 可口可樂 (= *Coca-Cola*)
Things go better with Coke. 有了可口可樂，食物更可口。
soft drink 清涼飲料；不含酒精的飲料

1. (**D**) 依句意，容易「被記得」，爲被動語態，故選 (D) *be*
   remembered。

2. (**D**) 這句標語是「來自」一則清涼飲料公司的廣告，選 (D) *from*。

But a good slogan or image is just the first step in effective advertising. The people who <u>create</u> ads follow a set of four
$\quad\quad\quad\quad\quad\quad\quad\quad\quad\quad\quad\quad\quad\quad\quad$ 3
principles, which are known <u>as</u> AIDA.
$\quad\quad\quad\quad\quad\quad\quad\quad\quad\quad\quad$ 4

不過好的廣告標語或是形象，只是有效廣告的第一步。製作廣告的人們都會遵守以下四個基本原則，也就是所謂的 AIDA。

** step〔stɛp〕*n.* 步驟　　effective〔ɪ'fɛktɪv〕*adj.* 有效的
advertising〔'ædvɚ͵taɪzɪŋ〕*n.* 廣告　　follow〔'fɑlo〕*v.* 遵守
a set of 一系列；一套　　principle〔'prɪnsəpl̩〕*n.* 原則

3.(**A**)　空格應填動詞，又依句意爲現在式，且爲主動語態，故選
　　　　(A) *create*〔krɪ'et〕*v.* 創造；製造。

4.(**A**)　依句意，選 (A) *be known as*「被稱爲」。而 (C) be known
　　　　to「被～知道」，(D) be known for「以～有名」，均不合
　　　　句意。

The "A" <u>stands for</u> attracting consumers' *attention*, the "I" and
　　　　　　　　5
"D" are for arousing their *interest* and *desire*, and the final "A"
is for encouraging them to take immediate *action*.
第一個 A 代表吸引消費者的「注意力」，而 I 跟 D 則是激起他們的「興
趣」跟「慾望」，最後一個 A 則是代表鼓勵他們採取立即的「行動」。

** attract〔ə'trækt〕*v.* 吸引　　consumer〔kən'sumɚ〕*n.* 消費者
attention〔ə'tɛnʃən〕*n.* 注意力
arouse〔ə'raʊz〕*v.* 激起；喚起　　interest〔'ɪntrɪst〕*n.* 興趣
desire〔dɪ'zaɪr〕*n.* 慾望；渴望
encourage〔ɪn'kɝɪdʒ〕*v.* 鼓勵　　*take action* 採取行動
immediate〔ɪ'midɪɪt〕*adj.* 立即的

5.(**C**)　(A) care for　喜歡；想要
　　　　(B) look for　尋找　　(C) *stand for*　代表
　　　　(D) stand out　突出；傑出

TEST 7

Read the following passage and choose the best answer for each blank from the choices below.

In daily interactions, we often need other people's help, and when we ___1___, it's important to know the correct way to ask for it. Making a request properly will not only determine if we actually obtain the help, but, more importantly, affect the attitude that people ___2___ toward us as well. Making requests, in other words, ___3___ an understanding of etiquette. The most polite requests generally use the expression "Would you mind ...?" or "Do you mind ...?" For example: "Would you mind ___4___? I can barely breathe." Requests ___5___ with "Would you" or "Could you" are slightly less formal, but still indirect and polite. Notice that these requests are still in the form of a question. 【中正高中】

1. (A) do   (B) take
   (C) make   (D) put

2. (A) held   (B) take
   (C) give   (D) put

3. (A) involve
   (B) are involved
   (C) has much to do with
   (D) do something about

4. (A) don't smoking here
   (B) if I smoke here
   (C) my smoking here
   (D) putting that thing out

5. (A) begin   (B) begun
   (C) beginning   (D) that are begun

TEST 7 詳解

In daily interactions, we often need other people's help, and when we <u>do</u>, it's important to know the correct way to
1
ask for it. Making a request properly will not only determine if we actually obtain the help, but, more importantly, affect the attitude that people <u>take</u> toward us as well.
2

我們在日常的互動當中，常會需要其他人的協助，而當我們需要幫助的時候，知道用正確的方法請求別人幫忙是很重要的。適當地提出請求，不僅能決定我們是否眞的能得到幫助，而且更重要的是，也會影響別人對我們的態度。

** daily〔'delɪ〕*adj.* 日常的；每天的
interaction〔ˌɪntə'ækʃən〕*n.* 交互作用；互動
ask for 要求　　request〔rɪ'kwɛst〕*n.* 要求；請求
properly〔'prɑpəlɪ〕*adv.* 適當地；正確地
determine〔dɪ'tɝmɪn〕*v.* 決定
actually〔'æktʃʊəlɪ〕*adv.* 眞地
obtain〔əb'ten〕*v.* 獲得
affect〔ə'fɛkt〕*v.* 影響　　attitude〔'ætəˌtjud〕*n.* 態度
toward〔tord〕*prep.* 對於　　***as well*** 也（= *too*）

1. (**A**) 依句意，空格應填入動詞片語 need other people's
   help，爲避免重複，可用助動詞 do 代替，故選 (A)。

2. (**B**) 表「抱持」…態度，動詞可用 hold 或 take，但依句意爲
   現在式，故 (A) held 不合，選 (B) ***take***。

Making requests, in other words, <u>has much to do with</u> an
                                                    3
understanding of etiquette. The most polite requests
generally use the expression "Would you mind …?" or
"Do you mind …?"

換句話說，提出請求和了解禮儀有很大的關係。最有禮貌的請求，
通常會使用「你是否介意…？」，或「你介意…嗎？」這樣的說法。

> ** *in other words* 換句話說
> understanding〔ˌʌndɚˈstændɪŋ〕*n.* 了解
> etiquette〔ˈɛtɪˌkɛt〕*n.* 禮儀
> polite〔pəˈlaɪt〕*adj.* 有禮貌的
> generally〔ˈdʒɛnərəlɪ〕*adv.* 通常
> expression〔ɪkˈsprɛʃən〕*n.* 說法
> mind〔maɪnd〕*v.* 介意

3. (**C**) 依句意，提出請求和了解禮儀「有很大的關連」，故選
(C) *has much to do with*。而 (A) involve「牽涉」和
(B) are involved，須改成 is involved in「和~有關」才
能選；(D) do something about「對~做些什麼；對~採
取行動」，則不合句意。

For example: "Would you mind <u>putting that thing out</u>? I
                                                  4
can barely breathe." Requests <u>beginning</u> with "Would you"
                                              5
or "Could you" are slightly less formal, but still indirect
and polite. Notice that these requests are still in the form
of a question.

例如：「你介意把那個東西熄滅嗎？我快要不能呼吸了。」用「你願意」或者「你能夠」作為開頭的要求，比較不那麼正式，但還是間接而且有禮貌的。要注意，這樣的請求依然是一種問句形式。

** barely〔'bɛrlɪ〕*adv.* 幾乎不　　breathe〔brið〕*v.* 呼吸
　　slightly〔'slaɪtlɪ〕*adv.* 稍微地
　　formal〔'fɔrml̩〕*adj.* 正式的
　　indirect〔͵ɪndə'rɛkt〕*adj.* 間接的
　　notice〔'notɪs〕*v.* 注意到　　form〔fɔrm〕*n.* 形式

4. (**D**) 依句意，選 (D) ***putting that thing out*** 「把那個東西熄滅」。　　***put out*** 熄滅（= *extinguish*）
而 (A) 須改成 not smoking here「不在這裡吸煙」，
(B) if I smoke here「如果我在這裡吸煙」和 (C) my smoking here「我在這裡吸煙」，則不合句意。

5. (**C**) 空格應填入關代和動詞 which begins 或 that begins，又關代 which 或 that 可省略，但動詞 begins 須改爲現在分詞 ***beginning***，故選 (C)。

───【劉毅老師的話】───
　　克漏字是各大考試的必考題型，非常重要。你一定要善用本書，把每道題目都徹底弄懂，記住「功夫下得深，鐵杵磨成針。」

TEST 8

Read the following passage and choose the best answer for each blank from the choices below.

About a hundred years ago, Europeans brought the accordion to the New World. Having begun as a __1__ organ, the accordion belongs to the ordinary people, out in the street and the public squares. Musical __2__ as the accordion is, it has been embraced by many cultures and __3__ to fit their own musical styles. __4__, Creole and African American influences gave birth to a new form of music called Cajun — a style of music with a __5__ rhythm and swinging sound different from the elegant waltzing style of the Old World. 【松山高中】

1. (A) vivid   (B) portable (C) cheerful   (D) symbolic

2. (A) suitcase (B) defense (C) immigrant (D) inspiration

3. (A) adapted   (B) adapting
   (C) adjust   (D) being adjusted

4. (A) However   (B) On the contrary
   (C) For example   (D) In other words

5. (A) defensive   (B) considerate
   (C) protective   (D) brisk

TEST 8 詳解

About a hundred years ago, Europeans brought the
accordion to the New World. Having begun as a <u>portable</u>
1
organ, the accordion belongs to the ordinary people, out in
the street and the public squares.

大約一百年前，歐洲人將手風琴帶到新世界。手風琴一開始是
種可手提的風琴，很適合一般大衆，在街上或是公共廣場上使用。

** European (ˌjʊrəˈpiən) *n.* 歐洲人
accordion (əˈkɔrdɪən) *n.* 手風琴
the New World 新世界；美洲大陸【或稱新大陸，相對於
舊大陸，是地理大發現後歐洲人對美洲大陸的統稱】
organ (ˈɔrgən) *n.* 風琴　　***belong to*** 屬於；適合
ordinary (ˈɔrdṇˌɛrɪ) *adj.* 一般的
ordinary people 一般民衆
square (skwɛr) *n.* 廣場

1. (**B**) 依句意，選 (B)***portable*** (ˈpɔrtəbḷ) *adj.* 可攜帶的；手
提式的。而 (A) vivid (ˈvɪvɪd) *adj.* 生動的；栩栩如生
的，(C) cheerful (ˈtʃɪrfəl) *adj.* 愉快的，(D) symbolic
(sɪmˈbɑlɪk) *adj.* 象徵性的，則不合句意。

Musical <u>immigrant</u> as the accordion is, it has been embraced
2
by many cultures and <u>adapted</u> to fit their own musical styles.
3

雖然手風琴是從國外引進的樂器，但卻被許多文化接受，並且將之改造成符合該文化本身的音樂風格。

　　** as〔æz〕*conj.* 雖然（= *though*）
　　　embrace〔ɪm'bres〕*v.* 擁抱；欣然接受
　　　fit〔fɪt〕*v.* 適合　　style〔staɪl〕*n.* 風格

2. (**C**)　依句意，選 (C) ***immigrant***〔'ɪməgrənt〕*n.* 移民；自國外引進的物品。而 (A) suitcase〔'sut͵kes〕*n.* 手提箱，(B) defense〔dɪ'fɛns〕*n.* 防禦，(D) inspiration〔͵ɪnspə'reʃən〕*n.* 靈感；激勵，則不合句意。

3. (**A**)　and 為對等連接詞，前面是過去分詞 embraced，空格也應填過去分詞，故選 (A) ***adapted***。
　　　adapt〔ə'dæpt〕*v.* 使適應；改造

For example, Creole and African American influences gave
　　　　4
birth to a new form of music called Cajun — a style of music
with a brisk rhythm and swinging sound different from the
　　　　5
elegant waltzing style of the Old World.
例如，克里奧爾人跟非裔美國人的影響，產生了一種叫作「卡金」的新音樂類型——這是種節奏輕快而且聲音美妙，不同於舊世界那種優雅的華爾茲的風格。

　　** Creole〔'kriol〕*adj.* 克里奧爾人的【美國南部的法國移民後裔】
　　　African American 非裔美國人的
　　　influence〔'ɪnfluəns〕*n.* 影響

give birth to 產生；造成　　form〔fɔrm〕*n.* 形式

Cajun〔'kedʒən〕*n.* 卡金【一種歐洲白人、黑人與印地安人的混雜文化，現存於路易西安納州與密西西比河三角洲一帶的特殊歷史文化】

rhythm〔'rɪðəm〕*n.* 韻律；節奏

swinging〔'swɪŋɪŋ〕*adj.* 節奏美妙的

be different from 和～不同

elegant〔'ɛləgənt〕*adj.* 優雅的

waltz〔wɔlts〕*v.* 跳華爾茲

the Old World 舊世界；歐洲（大陸）【即地理大發現前，歐洲人所知的世界】

4.（**C**）依句意，選 (C) *For example*「例如」。而 (A) however「然而」，(B) on the contrary「相反地」，(D) in other words「換句話說」，則不合句意。

5.（**D**）(A) defensive〔dɪ'fɛnsɪv〕*adj.* 防禦性的

(B) considerate〔kən'sɪdərɪt〕*adj.* 體貼的

(C) protective〔prə'tɛktɪv〕*adj.* 保護的

(D) *brisk*〔brɪsk〕*adj.* 輕快的

【劉毅老師的話】

　　成為克漏字答題高手並不難，只要你有決心、有毅力，就沒有任何事能阻礙你。

TEST 9

Read the following passage and choose the best answer for each blank from the choices below.

Can shyness be entirely got rid of or ___1___ reduced? Luckily, people can overcome shyness ___2___ patient effort in building self-confidence. For one thing, you have to accept not only your personal strengths ___3___ your weaknesses. As self-acceptance grows, shyness naturally decreases. For another thing, you don't have to waste time and energy ___4___ guilt and shame. If you have hurt someone's feelings, feeling ashamed achieves nothing. ___5___, accept the fact and make up your mind to be more sensitive in the future. 【成淵高中】

1. (A) at last   (B) at first   (C) at least   (D) at best

2. (A) by   (B) of   (C) at   (D) with

3. (A) as well   (B) but   (C) or   (D) so

4. (A) in   (B) at   (C) on   (D) with

5. (A) However   (B) Also
   (C) Nevertheless   (D) Instead

TEST 9 詳解

Can shyness be entirely got rid of or <u>at least</u> reduced?
1

Luckily, people can overcome shyness <u>with</u> patient effort in
2

building self-confidence.

　　能完全擺脫害羞，或至少降低害羞的程度嗎？幸好，人們能夠藉
由耐心的努力，建立自信心，克服害羞。

　　** shyness〔'ʃaɪnɪs〕*n.* 害羞　　entirely〔ɪn'taɪrlɪ〕*adv.* 完全地
　　get rid of 擺脫；除去　　reduce〔rɪ'djus〕*v.* 減少；降低
　　luckily〔'lʌkɪlɪ〕*adv.* 幸好　　overcome〔͵ovə'kʌm〕*v.* 克服
　　self-confidence〔'sɛlf'kɑnfədəns〕*n.* 自信

1. (**C**)　依句意，選 (C) ***at least***「至少」。而 (A) at last「最後；終
　　　　　於」，(B) at first「起初」，(D) at best「充其量」，均不
　　　　　合句意。

2. (**D**)　表「用～」，介系詞用 ***with***，選 (D)。

For one thing, you have to accept not only your personal
strengths <u>but</u> your weaknesses.　As self-acceptance grows,
3

shyness naturally decreases.

首先，你不只要接受自己的優點，也必須接受自己的缺點。當你越
能接受自己時，害羞自然就會減少了。

　　** ***for one thing*** 首先　　accept〔ək'sɛpt〕*v.* 接受
　　personal〔'pɝsn̩l〕*adj.* 個人的　　strength〔strɛŋθ〕*n.* 優點
　　weakness〔'wiknɪs〕*n.* 缺點

self-acceptance〔'sɛlfək'sɛptəns〕*n.* 自我接納

grow〔gro〕*v.* 成長;增加

naturally〔'nætʃərəlɪ〕*adv.* 自然地

decrease〔dɪ'kris〕*v.* 減少

3.(**B**) *not only…but (also)* ~　不僅…而且~

For another thing, you don't have to waste time and energy on
⎯⎯
4

guilt and shame.　If you have hurt someone's feelings, feeling

ashamed achieves nothing.　Instead, accept the fact and make
⎯⎯⎯⎯⎯
5

up your mind to be more sensitive in the future.

其次,你不必浪費時間和精力在罪惡感與羞愧上。如果你傷害了別人

的感情,覺得羞愧並不會有任何幫助。相反地,接受事實並下定決心,

以後感受要更敏銳一點。

** *for another thing* 其次　　energy〔'ɛnədʒɪ〕*n.* 精力

guilt〔gɪlt〕*n.* 罪惡感　　shame〔ʃem〕*n.* 羞愧;慚愧

ashamed〔ə'ʃemd〕*adj.* 感到慚愧的

achieve〔ə'tʃiv〕*v.* 達成　　*make up* one's *mind* 下定決心

sensitive〔'sɛnsətɪv〕*adj.* 敏感的;感受敏銳的

4.(**C**)　waste + 時間/金錢/精力 + { on + N
in + V-ing

其後的 guilt 和 shame 都是名詞,故選 (C) *on*。

5.(**D**)　依句意,選 (D) *Instead*「取而代之;相反地」。而 (A)

however「然而」,(B) also「而且;此外」,(C) nevertheless

〔,nɛvə-ðə'lɛs〕*adv.* 然而;儘管如此,均不合句意。

TEST 10

Read the following passage and choose the best answer for each
blank from the choices below.

In Okinawa, stone or wooden lion-dogs are
common. ____1____ tourists with their strange
stares, they stand guard at entrances or on rooftops.
____2____ their bizarre looks, they are honored for
protecting the islanders from invasion for centuries.

Festivals are also important traditions in
Okinawa, and they ____3____ the Okinawans' respect
for their ancestors. During ____4____ festivals,
Okinawans wear traditional clothes. The costumes
are durable and beautiful, and they represent the
island's ____5____. 【松山高中】

1. (A) Surrounding   (B) Surrounded
   (C) To surround   (D) To be surround

2. (A) Despite   (B) Though
   (C) As if   (D) In spite

3. (A) reveal   (B) starve
   (C) determine   (D) overlook

4. (A) loyal   (B) fierce
   (C) annual   (D) ideal

5. (A) response   (B) procession
   (C) fantasy   (D) heritage

TEST 10 詳解

In Okinawa, stone or wooden lion-dogs are common.
<u>Surrounding</u> tourists with their strange stares, they stand guard
    1
at entrances or on rooftops. <u>Despite</u> their bizarre looks, they are
            2
honored for protecting the islanders from invasion for centuries.

在沖繩，石頭或是木製的招福獅隨處可見。招福獅就守在入口或
屋頂上，用古怪的眼神來包圍遊客。儘管它們有著奇怪的外表，幾個
世紀以來，它們以保護島民不受入侵而受人尊敬。

  ** Okinawa〔͵okɪˋnɑwə〕n. 沖繩【日本琉球群島中最大的島嶼】

wooden〔ˋwʊdn̩〕adj. 木製的

lion-dog〔ˋlaɪənˏdɔg〕n. 沖繩招福獅【在沖繩方言中叫作 shisa，
    意思就是像獅子一樣的狗，自古相傳是保佑沖繩風調雨順的神獸】

stare〔stɛr〕n. 凝視；瞪視   guard〔gɑrd〕n. 守衛

stand guard 監視；看守   entrance〔ˋɛntrəns〕n. 入口

rooftop〔ˋrufˏtɑp〕n. 屋頂   bizarre〔bɪˋzɑr〕adj. 奇怪的

looks〔lʊks〕n. pl. 外表   honor〔ˋɑnɚ〕v. 尊敬

islander〔ˋaɪləndɚ〕n. 島上居民   invasion〔ɪnˋveʒən〕n. 入侵

1. (**A**) 原句為：***They*** surround tourists with…, ***and*** stand
    guard…，分詞構句可代替對等子句，但須放在主詞前面，
    故可簡化為：***Surrounding*** tourists…, ***they*** stand…。
    【詳見「文法寶典」p.459】

2. (**A**) 因 their bizarre looks 為名詞片語，故空格應填介系詞，
    而 (B) Though「雖然」，(C) As if「就好像」是連接詞，
    在此不合，而 (D) 須改為 In spite of「儘管」，才能選，故
    選 (A) ***Despite***「儘管」(= *In spite of*)。

Festivals are also important traditions in Okinawa, and they
<u>reveal</u> the Okinawans' respect for their ancestors. During <u>annual</u>
  3   4
festivals, Okinawans wear traditional clothes. The costumes are
durable and beautiful, and they represent the island's <u>heritage</u>.
                                                                 5

慶典也是沖繩重要的傳統，可顯示沖繩人對祖先的敬意。在一年
一度的慶典中，沖繩人會穿上傳統的服飾。這些服飾耐穿又美麗，而
且代表島上的文化遺產。

** festival (ˈfɛstəvḷ) *n.* 節慶　　tradition (trəˈdɪʃən) *n.* 傳統
Okinawan (ˌokɪˈnɑwən) *n.* 沖繩人
respect (rɪˈspɛkt) *n.* 敬意　　ancestor (ˈænsɛstɚ) *n.* 祖先
traditional (trəˈdɪʃənḷ) *adj.* 傳統的
costume (ˈkɑstjum) *n.* 服裝　　durable (ˈdjʊrəbḷ) *adj.* 耐用的
represent (ˌrɛprɪˈzɛnt) *v.* 代表

3. (**A**)　依句意，選 (A) ***reveal*** (rɪˈvil) *v.* 顯示。而 (B) starve
(stɑrv) *v.* 飢餓，(C) determine (dɪˈtɝmɪn) *v.* 決定，
(D) overlook (ˌovɚˈlʊk) *v.* 忽視，則不合句意。

4. (**C**)　(A) loyal (ˈlɔɪəl) *adj.* 忠實的
(B) fierce (fɪrs) *adj.* 兇猛的
(C) ***annual*** (ˈænjʊəl) *adj.* 一年一度的
(D) ideal (aɪˈdiəl) *adj.* 理想的

5. (**D**)　(A) response (rɪˈspɑns) *n.* 回應；反應
(B) procession (prəˈsɛʃən) *n.* 行列；行進
(C) fantasy (ˈfæntəsɪ) *n.* 幻想
(D) ***heritage*** (ˈhɛrətɪdʒ) *n.* 遺產

TEST 11

Read the following passage and choose the best answer for each blank from the choices below.

The Eiffel Tower was built for the International

Exhibition of Paris of 1889, ____1____ the centenary

of the French Revolution. The Prince of Wales,

later King Edward VII of England, opened the

tower. Of the 700 proposals ____2____ in a design

competition, Gustave Eiffel's was unanimously

chosen. ____3____, it was not accepted by all at

first, ____4____ a petition of 300 names — including

____5____ of Maupassant, Emile Zola, Charles

Garnier (architect of the Opéra Garnier), and

Dumas the Younger — protested its construction.

【師大附中】

1. (A) commemorate

   (B) commemorates

   (C) commemorated

   (D) which commemorated

2. (A) submit   (B) submits

   (C) submitted   (D) submitting

3. (A) However   (B) Therefore

   (C) Although   (D) Moreover

4. (A) and   (B) but

   (C) while   (D) which

5. (A) one   (B) ones

   (C) that   (D) those

TEST 11 詳解

The Eiffel Tower was built for the International Exhibition of Paris of 1889, <u>which commemorated</u> the centenary of the

1
French Revolution. The Prince of Wales, later King Edward VII of England, opened the tower.

艾菲爾鐵塔，是爲了 1889 年巴黎的世界博覽會而建造的，而這場博覽會，是爲了紀念法國大革命滿一百週年。英國當時的威爾斯親王，也就是後來的英皇愛德華七世，替鐵塔舉行揭幕典禮。

** Eiffel Tower〔'aɪfḷ'tauə〕 *n.* 艾菲爾鐵塔【1889 年建於巴黎，
  高 300 公尺】

be built for 爲了…目的而建造

international〔ˌɪntə'næʃənḷ〕 *adj.* 國際的

exhibition〔ˌɛksə'bɪʃən〕 *n.* 展覽會

International Exhibition 世界博覽會

centenary〔'sɛntəˌnɛrɪ〕 *n.* 百年紀念

revolution〔ˌrɛvə'luʃən〕 *n.* 革命

the French Revolution 法國大革命【1789-1799 年期間，
  法國人民因不滿君主統治政體而發起的革命運動】

prince〔prɪns〕 *n.* 王子；小國的君主

Wales〔welz〕 *n.* 威爾斯【英國西南部地區名】

the Prince of Wales 威爾斯親王【英國皇太子的封號】

later〔'letə〕 *adj.* 後來的

King Edward VII of England 英皇愛德華七世【1841-1910，
  英國維多利亞女皇的長子，在位期間，英法關係有長足進步】

open〔'opən〕 *v.* 爲…舉行揭幕典禮

1. (**D**) 空格應填關代，引導形容詞子句，修飾先行詞 the International Exhibition of Paris of 1889，且依句意為過去式，故用過去式動詞，選 (D) *which commemorated*。
commemorate〔kə'mɛmə,ret〕*v.* 紀念

Of the 700 proposals <u>submitted</u> in a design competition,
                              2
Gustave Eiffel's was unanimously chosen.
在設計比賽所提交的七百多個提案中，古斯塔夫・艾菲爾的設計，
得到眾人一致的認可而獲選。

    ** proposal〔prə'pozl̩〕*n.* 提議；提案
       competition〔,kɑmpə'tɪʃən〕*n.* 比賽
       Gustave Eiffel〔gju'stɑv'aɪfl̩〕*n.* 古斯塔夫・艾菲爾
       【艾菲爾鐵塔的建築設計師】
       unanimously〔ju'nænəməslɪ〕*adv.* 全體一致地

2. (**C**) Of the 700 proposals submitted in…是由 Of the 700 proposals *which were* submitted in…省略關代及 be 動詞簡化而來。
submit〔səb'mɪt〕*v.* 提交；提出

<u>However</u>, it was not accepted by all at first, <u>and</u> a petition of
    3   4
300 names — including <u>those</u> of Maupassant, Emile Zola,
                                    5
Charles Garnier (architect of the Opéra Garnier), and Dumas
the Younger — protested its construction.

然而，起初他的設計並沒有被所有人接受，一份三百人簽名的陳情書
——包括知名作家莫泊桑、埃米爾・左拉、加尼葉歌劇院的建築師查
理斯・加尼葉，還有小仲馬——都簽名抗議建造這個建築物。

** ***at first*** 起初　　petition〔pəˋtɪʃən〕*n.* 陳情書；請願書

Maupassant〔ˋmopəˏsɑnt〕*n.* 莫泊桑【1850-1893，法國知名作家】

Emile Zola〔ˋimɪlˋzolə〕*n.* 埃米爾・左拉【1840-1902，法國
　　知名作家及思想家】

Charles Garnier〔ˋtʃɑrlzˏgɑrˋnje〕*n.* 查理斯・加尼葉
　　【1825-1898，巴黎歌劇院的建築師】

architect〔ˋɑrkəˏtɛkt〕*n.* 建築師

Opéra Garnier〔ˋɑpərəˏgɑrˋnje〕*n.* 加尼葉歌劇院
　　【也就是知名的巴黎歌劇院，於 1875 年完工】

Dumas the Younger〔djuˋmɑˏðəˋjʌŋgɚ〕*n.* 小仲馬
　　【1824-1895，法國小說家及劇作家，全名 Alexandre Dumas】

protest〔prəˋtɛst〕*v.* 抗議；堅決聲明

construction〔kənˋstrʌkʃən〕*n.* 建造

3. (**A**)　依句意，選 (A) ***However***「然而」。而 (B) Therefore「因
　　　　此」，(C) Although「雖然」，(D) Moreover「此外」，
　　　　均不合句意。

4. (**A**)　空格應填連接詞，且句意並無轉折，故選 (A) ***and***「而且」。

5. (**D**)　為避免重複前面提過的名詞，單數可用 that 代替，複數則用
　　　　those 代替，故選 (D) ***those*** (= *the names*)。

TEST 12

Read the following passage and choose the best answer for each blank from the choices below.

The idea of skysurfing arose from a ___1___ thought, and it later proved ___2___. A skydiver jumped out of an airplane while wearing a board on his feet, ___3___ caught the wind in interesting ways. The skydiver could "surf" on the wind, ___4___ much more freely than a traditional skydiver. Of course, since skysurfing first appeared, many other tricks have been performed and this particular sport is sure to keep ___5___ the attention of those who are always looking for a new thrill. 【延平高中】

1. (A) satin   (B) random   (C) curtain   (D) ransom

2. (A) successful   (B) successfully
   (C) success   (D) succeed

3. (A) that   (B) which   (C) for   (D) to

4. (A) strapping   (B) expatriating
   (C) submitting   (D) maneuvering

5. (A) attracting   (B) assuming
   (C) appealing   (D) awarding

TEST 12 詳解

The idea of skysurfing arose from a <u>random</u> thought, and it
                                           1
later proved <u>successful</u>.
             2

　　空中滑板運動的概念，來自於一個隨機的想法，這個想法之後被
證明是成功的。

> ** skysurfing〔'skaɪ,sɜfɪŋ〕*n.* 空中滑板【一種極限運動，跳傘的
> 　　一種，但腳上穿著滑板，就像在空中衝浪或滑雪一樣】
> 　　arise〔ə'raɪz〕*v.* 出現；發生　　***arise from*** 起源於
> 　　prove〔pruv〕*v.* 證明是；（結果）成為

1. (**B**)　(A) satin〔'sætɪn〕*n.* 緞
　　　　　　(B) ***random***〔'rændəm〕*adj.* 隨便的；隨機的
　　　　　　(C) curtain〔'kɜtn̩〕*n.* 窗簾
　　　　　　(D) ransom〔'rænsəm〕*n.* 贖金

2. (**A**)　prove 作「證明是；（結果）成為」解時，其後須接形容詞，
　　　　　　故選 (A) ***successful***「成功的」。而 (B) successfully
　　　　　　〔sək'sɛsfəlɪ〕*adv.* 成功地，(C) success〔sək'sɛs〕*n.* 成功，
　　　　　　(D) succeed〔sək'sid〕*v.* 成功，用法均不合。

A skydiver jumped out of an airplane while wearing a board
on his feet, <u>which</u> caught the wind in interesting ways.　The
　　　　　　　3
skydiver could "surf" on the wind, <u>maneuvering</u> much more
　　　　　　　　　　　　　　　　　　　4
freely than a traditional skydiver.

跳傘者從飛機上跳下來，同時在腳上穿著一塊板子，板子能以有趣的方
法乘著風。跳傘者能乘風「衝浪」，能比傳統的跳傘者更自由地移動。

** skydiver〔'skaɪ,daɪvɚ〕*n.* 跳傘者　　jump〔dʒʌmp〕*v.* 跳
jump out of 從…跳下　　board〔bord〕*n.* 木板
catch the wind　（船等）鼓滿風；乘風
surf〔sɝf〕*v.* 衝浪　　traditional〔trə'dɪʃənl〕*adj.* 傳統的

3. (**B**)　空格應填關係代名詞，代替先行詞 a board，又前有逗點，
　　　　不能用 that，故選 (B) ***which***。

4. (**D**)　(A) strap〔stræp〕*v.* 用皮帶綁
　　　　(B) expatriate〔ɛks'petrɪ,et〕*v.* 把…放逐到國外
　　　　(C) submit〔səb'mɪt〕*v.* 屈服；提出
　　　　(D) ***maneuver***〔mə'nuvɚ〕*v.* 移動

Of course, since skysurfing first appeared, many other tricks have
been performed and this particular sport is sure to keep <u>attracting</u>
$\qquad\qquad\qquad\qquad\qquad\qquad\qquad\qquad\qquad\qquad\qquad\qquad$ 5
the attention of those who are always looking for a new thrill.
當然，自從空中滑板出現之後，表演了很多種不同的特技，而且這種
特殊的運動，一定能持續吸引那些，一直尋求新刺激的人的注意。

** first〔fɝst〕*adv.* 最初　　appear〔ə'pɪr〕*v.* 出現
trick〔trɪk〕*n.* 特技；把戲　　perform〔pɚ'fɔrm〕*v.* 表演
particular〔pɚ'tɪkjəlɚ〕*adj.* 特別的；獨特的
be sure to 必定　　attention〔ə'tɛnʃən〕*n.* 注意力
thrill〔θrɪl〕*n.* 刺激；興奮

5. (**A**)　(A) ***attract***〔ə'trækt〕*v.* 吸引（= *appeal to*）
　　　　(B) assume〔ə'sum〕*v.* 認為
　　　　(C) appeal〔ə'pil〕*v.* 吸引（為不及物動詞，須加 to 才能選）
　　　　(D) award〔ə'wɔrd〕*v.* 頒發

TEST 13

Read the following passage and choose the best answer for each blank from the choices below.

People have for centuries recognized the power of luck and have tried all means to seize it. ___1___, they might follow some old superstitions ___2___ to ancient times ___3___ people asked for help from supernatural powers. A psychologist conducted a 10-year study to investigate why some people are consistently lucky while others ___4___. She advertised in national periodicals ___5___ volunteers, and people from all walks of life — ___6___ 18 to 84 — responded. She asked these ___7___ to complete diaries, personality questionnaires, and IQ tests. Her research indicates that the key to ___8___ lucky lies in three basic principles: seizing opportunities, creating ___9___ prophecies through positive expectations, and developing flexibility that ___10___ bad luck. 【板橋高中】

1. (A) In contrast   (B) On the contrary
   (C) For example   (D) On average

2. (A) dating back   (B) dated back
   (C) go back   (D) tracing back

3. (A) where   (B) that
   (C) when   (D) why

4. (A) don't   (B) aren't
   (C) weren't   (D) didn't

5. (A) with   (B) concerning
   (C) for   (D) by means of

6. (A) aged   (B) age
   (C) old   (D) aging

7. (A) predictions   (B) subjects
   (C) techniques   (D) adjustments

8. (A) be   (B) been
   (C) being   (D) is

9. (A) self-fulfill   (B) self-fulfilled
   (C) self-fulfilling   (D) self-fulfillments

10. (A) turns around   (B) carries out
    (C) looks around   (D) dwells on

TEST 13 詳解

People have for centuries recognized the power of luck and have tried all means to seize it. <u>For example</u>, they might follow
1

some old superstitions <u>dating back</u> to ancient times <u>when</u> people
2   3

asked for help from supernatural powers.

　　幾個世紀以來，人們都認同運氣的力量，而且用盡一切方法想抓住好運。例如，當人們請求超自然力量的幫助時，可能會遵從某些可追溯至古代的迷信。

** century〔'sɛntʃərɪ〕*n.* 世紀
recognize〔'rɛkəg,naɪz〕*v.* 承認；認同
luck〔lʌk〕*n.* 好運；運氣
means〔minz〕*n.* 方法；手段【單複數同形】
seize〔siz〕*v.* 抓住；把握　　follow〔'fɑlo〕*v.* 遵守
superstition〔,supə'stɪʃən〕*n.* 迷信
ancient〔'enʃənt〕*adj.* 古代的　　***ancient times*** 古代
ask for 要求　　supernatural〔,supə'nætʃərəl〕*adj.* 超自然的

1. (**C**)　(A) in contrast　對比之下
　　　　　　(B) on the contrary　相反地
　　　　　　(C) ***for example***　例如
　　　　　　(D) on average　平均而言

2. (**A**)　原句爲：…some old superstitions ***which dated back*** to
　　　　　ancient times…，可省略關代 which，且將動詞 dated 改
　　　　　爲現在分詞 dating，故選 (A) ***dating back***。
　　　　　date back to　追溯至 (= *be traced back to*)

3. (**C**)　表時間，關係副詞用 ***when***，選 (C)。

A psychologist conducted a 10-year study to investigate why
some people are consistently lucky while others <u>aren't</u>.　She
　　　　　　　　　　　　　　　　　　　　　　　　4
advertised in national periodicals <u>for</u> volunteers, and people
　　　　　　　　　　　　　　　　5
from all walks of life — <u>aged</u> 18 to 84 — responded.
　　　　　　　　　　　　6
有位心理學家做了長達十年的研究，調查為什麼有些人一直都很幸
運，而有些人卻沒有那樣的好運。她在全國性的期刊上登廣告，徵求
自願者，而各行各業的人，年齡在十八至八十四歲之間，都回覆她。

　** psychologist〔saɪˈkɑlədʒɪst〕*n.* 心理學家
　　conduct〔kənˈdʌkt〕*v.* 進行；做　　　study〔ˈstʌdɪ〕*n.* 研究
　　investigate〔ɪnˈvɛstəˌget〕*v.* 調查
　　consistently〔kənˈsɪstəntlɪ〕*adv.* 經常；一直
　　advertise〔ˈædvɚˌtaɪz〕*v.* 刊登廣告
　　periodical〔ˌpɪrɪˈɑdɪkḷ〕*n.* 定期刊物
　　volunteer〔ˌvɑlənˈtɪr〕*n.* 自願者
　　all walks of life 各行各業　　respond〔rɪˈspɑnd〕*v.* 回應

4. (**B**)　有些人「不是」一直都很幸運，且依句意為現在式，故選
　　　　 (B) ***aren't***。

5. (**C**)　在期刊上登廣告，「為了」要找自願者，選 (C) ***for***。而 (A)
　　　　 with「和～一起」，(B) concerning「關於」，(D) by
　　　　 means of「藉由」，均不合句意。

6. (**A**)　表「～歲的」，須用「***aged*** + 數字」，故選 (A)。而 (D)
　　　　 aging「老化」，則不合句意。

She asked these <u>subjects</u> to complete diaries, personality
                7

questionnaires, and IQ tests. Her research indicates that the

key to <u>being</u> lucky lies in three basic principles: seizing
       8

opportunities, creating <u>self-fulfilling</u> prophecies through
               9

positive expectations, and developing flexibility that

<u>turns around</u> bad luck.
   10

她要求這些研究對象完成日記、性格問卷調查，與智力測驗。她的研
究指出，幸運的關鍵在於三個基本原則：抓住機會、透過正面的期待
創造出自我實現的預言，並培養可以反轉惡運的靈活性。

   ** complete〔kəm'plit〕*v.* 完成

       diary〔'daɪərɪ〕*n.* 日記

       personality〔,pɜsn̩'ælətɪ〕*n.* 個性

       questionnaire〔,kwɛstʃən'ɛr〕*n.* 問卷

       IQ 智商（ = *intelligence quotient*）

       IQ test 智力測驗   research〔'risɜtʃ〕*n.* 研究

       indicate〔'ɪndə,ket〕*v.* 指出

       the key to ~ ~的關鍵   *lie in* 在於

       principle〔'prɪnsəpl̩〕*n.* 原則

       opportunity〔,apə'tjunətɪ〕*n.* 機會

       create〔krɪ'et〕*v.* 創造   prophecy〔'prafəsɪ〕*n.* 預言

       positive〔'pazətɪv〕*adj.* 正面的；積極的

       expectation〔,ɛkspɛk'teʃən〕*n.* 期望；預期

       develop〔dɪ'vɛləp〕*v.* 培養

       flexibility〔,flɛksə'bɪlətɪ〕*n.* 靈活度   *bad luck* 惡運

7. (**B**)　(A) prediction〔prɪˈdɪkʃən〕*n.* 預測

(B) ***subject***〔ˈsʌbdʒɪkt〕*n.* 實驗對象

(C) technique〔tɛkˈnik〕*n.* 技術

(D) adjustment〔əˈdʒʌstmənt〕*n.* 調整

8. (**C**)　the key to「~ 的關鍵」中的 to 是介系詞，其後須接名詞或動名詞，故選 (C) ***being***。

9. (**C**)　依句意，創造出正面的「自我實現的」預言，選 (C) ***self-fulfilling*** *adj.* 自我實現的；充分發揮自己潛在能力的。而 (A) self-fulfill〔ˌsɛlfʊlˈfɪl〕*v.* 自我實現；實現自己的願望，(B) self-fulfilled *adj.* 已經自我實現的，(D) self-fulfillment *n.* 自我實現，用法與句意均不合。

10. (**A**)　培養可以「反轉」惡運的靈活度，選 (A) ***turns around*** 「使倒轉；使好轉；轉變」。而 (B) carry out「實行」，(C) look around「環顧四周」，(D) dwell on「老是想著」，均不合句意。

TEST 14

Read the following passage and choose the best answer for each blank from the choices below.

Game shows are among the most entertaining programs on the air today. Millions of people ___1___ these shows, their eyes ___2___ to the TV until the final question is answered and there is a winner. In *Jeopardy*, however, three contestants have to figure out the correct question ___3___ give the right answer. In *Komodo Dragon*, the craziest game show in Japan, people tie raw meat ___4___ their heads and then put their heads into a glass box with a Komodo dragon inside. The last person standing there with the dragon wins! Suspense, therefore, is created as luck ___5___ a more important ___5___ than knowledge or skill does.

【大同高中】

1. (A) tune in to   (B) watch out

   (C) compete against   (D) make up

2. (A) haunted   (B) concerned

   (C) paralyzed   (D) glued

3. (A) in addition   (B) rather than

   (C) despite   (D) instead of

4. (A) in   (B) at

   (C) from   (D) on

5. (A) puts ; spin   (B) does ; research

   (C) has ; access   (D) plays ; role

TEST 14 詳解

Game shows are among the most entertaining programs
on the air today. Millions of people <u>tune in to</u> these shows,
1
their eyes <u>glued</u> to the TV until the final question is
2
answered and there is a winner.

益智節目是目前播出的節目中，最具娛樂效果的節目。數百
萬民眾收看這些節目，他們眼睛緊盯著電視，直到最後一個問題
被回答出來，產生優勝者為止。

** game〔gem〕*n.* 比賽；遊戲　　show〔ʃo〕*n.* 節目
game shows 益智節目
entertaining〔͵ɛntə'tenɪŋ〕*adj.* 具娛樂效果的；有趣的
program〔'progræm〕*n.* 節目　　***on the air*** 播映中

1. (**A**) 依句意，選 (A) ***tune in to***「收看；收聽」。而 (B)
watch out「注意」，(C) compete against「和～競
爭」(= *compete with*)，(D) make up「編造；組
成」，均不合句意。

2. (**D**) glue〔glu〕*v.* 用膠水黏
be glued to sth. 目不轉睛地盯著某物
one's eyes glued to the TV 目不轉睛地盯著電視
(A) haunted〔'hɔntɪd〕*adj.* 有鬼魂出沒的，(B) concern
〔kən'sɜn〕*v.* 關心，(C) paralyze〔'pærə͵laɪz〕*v.* 使麻
痺，均不合句意。

In *Jeopardy*, however, three contestants have to figure out
the correct question <u>rather than</u> give the right answer.
                                    3
不過,在美國節目「危險」當中,三位參賽者必須要想出正確的
問題,而不是回答正確的答案。

    ** Jeopardy〔ˈdʒɛpɚdɪ〕 *n.* 危險【此為美國的一個益智節目,
       特別之處在於參賽者由答案中,猜出問題是什麼】
       contestant〔kənˈtɛstənt〕 *n.* 參賽者
       figure out 想出;算出

  3. (**B**) 依句意,要想出正確的問題,「而不是」說出正確的答
       案,選 (B) *rather than*「而不是」。而 (A) in addition
       「此外」,(C) despite「儘管」,不合句意;(D) instead
       of「而不是」,其後須接名詞或動名詞,在此用法不合。

In *Komodo Dragon*, the craziest game show in Japan, people
tie raw meat <u>on</u> their heads and then put their heads into a
         4
glass box with a Komodo dragon inside. The last person
standing there with the dragon wins! Suspense, therefore,
is created as luck <u>plays</u> a more important <u>role</u> than knowledge
          5   5
or skill does.
在日本最瘋狂的益智節目「科摩多龍」中,人們在頭上綁著生肉,
然後把頭放到裡面有科摩多龍的玻璃箱中。最後一個跟科摩多龍
站在一起的人就是贏家!因此,由於運氣扮演的角色,比知識或
技巧都還來得重要,所以就能製造出緊張懸疑的氣氛。

** Komodo〔kə'modo〕*n.* 科摩多【印尼小島名】

dragon〔'drægən〕*n.* 龍

Komodo Dragon 科摩多龍【產於印尼科摩多島的巨型

　蜥蜴，全長 3.5 公尺，是世界上最大的蜥蜴。日本益智節

　目即以此為名。】

tie〔taɪ〕*v.* 繫著；綁住　　raw〔rɔ〕*adj.* 生的

suspense〔sə'spɛns〕*n.* 懸疑；緊張

create〔krɪ'et〕*v.* 創造　　luck〔lʌk〕*n.* 運氣

knowledge〔'nɑlɪdʒ〕*n.* 知識　　skill〔skɪl〕*n.* 技巧

4.(**D**) 依句意，表「在⋯上面」，介系詞用 *on*，選 (D)。

5.(**D**) 依句意，選 (D) ***plays a more important role***「扮演

　　一個比較重要的角色」。而 (A) spin〔spɪn〕*n.* 旋轉，

　　(B) research〔'risɝtʃ〕*n.* 研究，(C) access〔'æksɛs〕

　　n. 接近或使用權，均不合句意。

```
───【劉毅老師的話】───
　　對文法不懂的地方，可查閱文
法寶典，徹底了解，例如 on 的用法
可查閱「文法寶典」p.591 頁。
```

TEST 15

Read the following passage and choose the best answer for each
blank from the choices below.

A GPS receiver is a compact device which can

tell you where you are. This ___1___ device can be

connected to a system of satellites. GPS receivers

are perfect for mountaineers. They let them ___2___

how high up they are. Some new cars, ___3___ with

GPS receivers, can even guide drivers.

1. (A) hand-holding   (B) hand-held
   (C) holding-hand   (D) held-hand

2. (A) poke   (B) marvel
   (C) know   (D) pluck

3. (A) accompany   (B) accompanying
   (C) to accompany   (D) equipped

They usually come with monitors that can display high-resolution maps. As the driver moves, the map ___4___ in the right direction. ___5___, with the help of a GPS receiver, people can locate a place much more easily. For example, fishermen can find where the nearest fishing lake is. In short, a GPS receiver is a wonderful device. 【松山高中】

4. (A) leaps   (B) scrolls

   (C) swirls   (D) glimpses

5. (A) Instead   (B) In addition

   (C) However   (D) Although

TEST 15 詳解

A GPS receiver is a compact device which can tell you where you are. This <u>hand-held</u> device can be connected to
1

a system of satellites. GPS receivers are perfect for mountaineers. They let them <u>know</u> how high up they are.
2

GPS 接收器是一個小型裝置，它能告訴你身處何處。這個手提式的裝置，能和衛星系統連結。GPS 接收器非常適合登山者使用。它們讓登山者知道自己在多高的位置。

** GPS 全球定位系統 (= *Global Positioning System*)
【一種連結衛星系統做出定位點的小型裝置，常見的像是車上衛星導航儀器】
receiver〔rɪ'sivɚ〕*n.* 接收器
compact〔kəm'pækt〕*adj.* 小型的
device〔dɪ'vaɪs〕*n.* 裝置　　*be connected to* 和…連結
satellite〔'sætḷ,aɪt〕*n.* 衛星　　*be perfect for* 非常適合
mountaineer〔,maʊntṇ'ɪr〕*n.* 登山者
high up 在極高處

1. (**B**) 依句意，選 (B) *hand-held*「手提式的」。

2. (**C**) 依句意，讓他們「知道」自己在多高的位置，選 (C) *know*。而 (A) poke〔pok〕*v.* 戳，(B) marvel〔'marvḷ〕*v.* 感到驚訝，(D) pluck〔plʌk〕*v.* 拔出；摘（花），均不合句意。

Some new cars, <u>equipped</u> with GPS receivers, can even
                     3

guide drivers. They usually come with monitors that can
display high-resolution maps. As the driver moves, the
map <u>scrolls</u> in the right direction.
      4

有些配備有 GPS 接收器的新車，甚至能當駕駛人的嚮導。它們通
常附有螢幕，能顯示高解析度的地圖。當駕駛人開動車子，地圖
會往正確的方向捲動。

> ** guide〔gaɪd〕*v.* 引導；當嚮導
> ***come with***　附有
> monitor〔'mɑnətɚ〕*n.*（電腦）顯示器
> display〔dɪ'sple〕*v.* 展示
> high-resolution〔'haɪˌrɛzə'luʃən〕*adj.* 高解析度的
> move〔muv〕*v.* 移動

3. (**D**)　依句意，「配備有」GPS 接收器，選 (D) ***equipped***
　　　　with。本句是由 Some new cars, which are
　　　　equipped with GPS receivers,…省略關代 which
　　　　和 be 動詞 are 簡化而來。而 (A) (B) (C) accompany
　　　　〔ə'kʌmpənɪ〕*v.* 陪伴，均不合句意。

4. (**B**)　(A) leap〔lip〕*v.* 跳
　　　　(B) ***scroll***〔skrol〕*v.* 捲動
　　　　(C) swirl〔swɝl〕*v.* 旋轉
　　　　(D) glimpse〔glɪmps〕*v.* 瞥見

<u>In addition</u>, with the help of a GPS receiver, people can
　　　5

locate a place much more easily.　For example, fishermen

can find where the nearest fishing lake is.　In short, a

GPS receiver is a wonderful device.

除此之外，有了 GPS 接收器的幫助，人們能更容易查出某地的位
置。例如，漁夫能找到最近的釣魚湖泊。簡言之，GPS 接收器是
個很棒的裝置。

　　** locate〔'loket〕*v.* 查出…的位置
　　　fishing〔'fɪʃɪŋ〕*adj.* 釣魚的
　　　in short 簡言之
　　　wonderful〔'wʌndɚfəl〕*adj.* 很棒的

5. (**B**) (A) instead〔ɪn'stɛd〕*adv.* 取而代之
　　　 (B) *in addition* 此外

$$\left\{\begin{array}{l} = \text{besides} \\ = \text{additionally} \\ = \text{what's more} \\ = \text{moreover} \\ = \text{furthermore} \end{array}\right.$$

　　　 (C) however〔hau'ɛvɚ〕*adv.* 然而
　　　 (D) although〔ɔl'ðo〕*conj.* 雖然

TEST 16

Read the following passage and choose the best answer for each blank from the choices below.

Religion was very important in the lives of the Australian aborigines. They had some religious stories ___1___ from their ancestors about the creation of the Earth, the stars, and the moon. In other words, they passed down their stories from one generation to ___2___. Through this oral tradition, these aborigines taught their youth the beliefs of their own tribes. Those beliefs were ___3___ their respect and admiration for Nature, to which they believed men would finally return after death. They called their religious stories the "dreaming" or the "dream time" ___4___ out the fact that they ___5___ the imagination and creativity in their traditions. 【中正高中】

1. (A) passed down   (B) fulfilled

    (C) balanced   (D) promised

2. (A) the others   (B) the next

    (C) another ones   (D) the rest

3. (A) ran out of   (B) found fault with

    (C) based on   (D) watered for

4. (A) point   (B) which for pointing

    (C) that point   (D) to point

5. (A) prided themselves on

    (B) proud of

    (C) took pride

    (D) had proud

TEST 16 詳解

Religion was very important in the lives of the
Australian aborigines. They had some religious stories
<u>passed down</u> from their ancestors about the creation of
　　　1
the Earth, the stars, and the moon. In other words, they
passed down their stories from one generation to <u>the next</u>.
　　　　　　　　　　　　　　　　　　　　　　　　　　　2

　　宗教在澳洲原住民的生活中非常重要。他們有一些宗教故
事,是關於地球的創造、星辰、月亮,是由祖先流傳下來的。
換句話說,他們會將這些故事代代相傳。

　　** religion〔rɪ'lɪdʒən〕*n.* 宗教
　　　　Australian〔ɔ'streljən〕*adj.* 澳洲的
　　　　aborigine〔͵æbə'rɪdʒəni〕*n.* 原住民
　　　　religious〔rɪ'lɪdʒəs〕*adj.* 宗教的
　　　　ancestor〔'ænsɛstɚ〕*n.* 祖先
　　　　creation〔krɪ'eʃən〕*n.* 創造
　　　　Earth〔ɝθ〕*n.* 地球　　　*in other words* 換句話說
　　　　pass down~ 把~往下傳
　　　　generation〔͵dʒɛnə'reʃən〕*n.* 世代

1.(**A**) 依句意,選 (A) ***passed down***「被往下傳」。而 (B)
　　　fulfill〔ful'fɪl〕*v.* 實現,(C) balance〔'bæləns〕*v.*
　　　使平衡,(D) promise〔'pramɪs〕*v.* 保證,皆不合
　　　句意。

2. (**B**) 依句意，選 (B) ***pass down ~ from one generation to the next*** 「把~代代相傳」。而 (A) the others「其餘的人或物」（= *the rest*），不合句意，(C) 無此用法。

Through this oral tradition, these aborigines taught their youth the beliefs of their own tribes. Those beliefs were <u>based on</u>
　　　　　　　　　　　　　　　　　　　　　　　　　　3
their respect and admiration for Nature, to which they believed men would finally return after death.
原住民藉由這種口述傳統，教導下一代有關他們部落的信仰。這些信仰是基於對大自然的尊敬跟景仰，他們相信人死後終究會回歸大自然。

　** oral〔'orəl〕*adj.* 口述的
　　tradition〔trə'dɪʃən〕*n.* 傳統　　youth〔juθ〕*n.* 年輕人
　　belief〔bɪ'lif〕*n.* 信仰　　tribe〔traɪb〕*n.* 部落
　　respect〔rɪ'spɛkt〕*n.* 尊敬；敬意
　　admiration〔͵ædmə'reʃən〕*n.* 欽佩；讚賞
　　Nature〔'netʃɚ〕*n.* 大自然

3. (**C**) 依句意，選 (C) ***be based on*** 「以~爲基礎」。而 (A) run out of「跑出；用完」，(B) find fault with「挑剔」，(D) water〔'wɔtɚ〕*v.* 澆水；流口水，則不合句意。

They called their religious stories the "dreaming" or the "dream time" <u>to point</u> out the fact that they <u>prided themselves on</u> the
　　　　　　　　　　4　　　　　　　　　　　　　　　　5
imagination and creativity in their traditions.

他們稱這些宗教故事為「做夢」，或「夢世紀」，來顯示他們對自己傳統中的想像力跟創造力非常自豪。

> ** dreaming〔'drimɪŋ〕*n.* 做夢
>
> ***dream time*** 夢世紀【澳洲原住民口述歷史中的遠古時代
> 傳說，他們認為高山是靜止的有袋類動物，河流是彩虹蛇
> 的足跡，銀河是天空之河，星星是河中反射的光芒】
> imagination〔ɪˌmædʒə'neʃən〕*n.* 想像力
> creativity〔ˌkrie'tɪvətɪ〕*n.* 創造力

4. (**D**)　不定詞 to V. 表示「目的」，故選 (D) ***to point***。

　　point out 指出

5. (**A**)　$\begin{cases} \textbf{\textit{pride}}\ oneself\ \textbf{\textit{on}} \\ = \text{take pride in} \\ = \text{be proud of} \end{cases}$

　　　　　　以～為榮

【劉毅老師的話】

　　學測和指考都會考克漏字測驗，按照歷年的出題方式來看，每篇克漏字的作答時間大概只有 3～5 分鐘，同學們平時練習時，最好是計時答題，訓練自己的作答速度。

TEST 17

Read the following passage and choose the best answer for each blank from the choices below.

Genetic engineering, the technology of changing certain genes in an organism, has ___1___ heated debate in recent years. Supporters embrace it because they could change the world any way they like — plants could be made bigger and more resistant ___2___ diseases and insects, for example. What's more fascinating is that parents could even customize their babies to suit their specific preferences,

1. (A) resulted in   (B) catered to
   (C) evolved from   (D) lasted for

2. (A) in   (B) on
   (C) at   (D) to

____3____ having larger eyes or whiter skin. ____4____,

some opponents disagree with the idea of playing

God on moral grounds. They argue that human

beings are in no position to decide the future for

other ____5____ on earth. 【成功高中】

3. (A) such as   (B) as well as
   (C) the same as   (D) known as

4. (A) Instead   (B) Gradually
   (C) Nevertheless   (D) Especially

5. (A) organs   (B) substances
   (C) beings   (D) tribes

TEST 17 詳解

　　Genetic engineering, the technology of changing certain genes in an organism, has <u>resulted in</u> heated debate in recent years.
　　　　　　　　　　　　　　　　　　　　　　1

　　基因工程學是種改變有機體內某些基因的科技，在最近幾年已經引發各界激烈的辯論。

** genetic ﹝ dʒəˈnɛtɪk ﹞ *adj.* 基因的；遺傳學的
　　engineering ﹝ˌɛndʒəˈnɪrɪŋ﹞ *n.* 工程學
　　technology ﹝ tɛkˈnɑlədʒɪ﹞ *n.* 科技
　　certain ﹝ˈsɝtn̩﹞ *adj.* 某些　　**gene** ﹝ dʒin﹞ *n.* 基因
　　organism ﹝ˈɔrgənˌɪzəm﹞ *n.* 有機體
　　heated ﹝ˈhitɪd﹞ *adj.* 激烈的
　　debate ﹝ dɪˈbet﹞ *n.* 辯論
　　recent ﹝ˈrisn̩t﹞ *adj.* 最近的

1. (**A**)　(A) ***result in*** 導致；造成
　　　　(B) cater to 迎合
　　　　(C) evolve from 從…演化而來
　　　　(D) last for 持續

　　Supporters embrace it because they could change the world any way they like — plants could be made bigger and more resistant <u>to</u> diseases and insects, for example.
　　　　　　　　　　　　2

支持者欣然接受這項技術，因為他們可以任意改變世界——例如，可以使植物長得更大，更能抵抗病蟲害。

** supporter〔sə'portɚ〕*n.* 支持者；擁護者
　　embrace〔ɪm'bres〕*v.* 擁抱；欣然接受
　　resistant〔rɪ'zɪstənt〕*adj.* 有抵抗力的
　　insect〔'ɪnsɛkt〕*n.* 昆蟲

2.(**D**) *be resistant to* 能抵抗～

What's more fascinating is that parents could even customize
their babies to suit their specific preferences, <u>such as</u> having
larger eyes or whiter skin.

3
更吸引人的是，父母能訂做自己的孩子，以符合自己特殊的喜好，
像是有較大的眼睛，或較白的皮膚。

** fascinating〔'fæsn̩ˌetɪŋ〕*adj.* 迷人的
　　customize〔'kʌstəmˌaɪz〕*v.* 訂做
　　suit〔sut〕*v.* 適合；配合
　　specific〔spɪ'sɪfɪk〕*adj.* 特定的
　　preference〔'prɛfərəns〕*n.* 偏好　　skin〔skɪn〕*n.* 皮膚

3.(**A**) 依句意，選(A) *such as*「像是」(= *like*)。而(B) as well
　　　　as「以及」，(C) the same as「和～一樣」，(D) be known
　　　　as「被稱為」，均不合句意。

<u>Nevertheless</u>, some opponents disagree with the idea of
4
playing God on moral grounds. They argue that human
beings are in no position to decide the future for other
<u>beings</u> on earth.
5

儘管如此，有些反對者基於道德的理由，不同意這種扮演上帝角
色的想法。反對者主張，人類沒有立場決定地球上其他生物的未
來。

> ** opponent〔ə'ponənt〕n. 反對者
> disagree〔,dɪsə'gri〕v. 不同意
> play〔ple〕v. 扮演　　moral〔'mɔrəl〕adj. 道德的
> ground〔graʊnd〕n. 理由
> argue〔'ɑrgju〕v. 主張　　**human beings** 人類
> position〔pə'zɪʃən〕n. 立場
> **be in no position to + V.** 沒有做～的立場

4. (**C**) 依句意，選 (C) **Nevertheless**「儘管如此」。而 (A)
   instead「取而代之；相反地」，(B) gradually
   〔'grædʒʊəlɪ〕adv. 逐漸地，(D) especially「尤其；
   特別是」，均不合句意。

5. (**C**) 人類沒有立場決定其他「生物」的未來，選 (C) **beings**
   〔'biɪŋz〕n. pl. 生物。而 (A) organ〔'ɔrgən〕n. 器官，
   (B) substance〔'sʌbstəns〕n. 物質，(D) tribe〔traɪb〕
   n. 部落，則不合句意。

TEST 18

*Read the following passage and choose the best answer for each
blank from the choices below.*

There is no accounting for tastes. One person's
meat may be another's poison. For example, insects,
candied or fried, are ___1___ mouth-watering foods
in some parts of the world, while in other regions
roasted mice are a delicacy. Likewise, Americans
may say that they are "___2___ to eat a horse," but if
___3___ horsemeat, which is actually eaten in some
areas of France, they would never try it.

In fact, a mixture of some factors ___4___ us to
choose certain foods. The geography of the country
has an important role in food selection. Millet is a
type of grain eaten in Africa, ___5___ is plentiful, but
in other places it is used as birdseed. 【北一女中】

1. (A) considered as   (B) looked upon

  (C) thought as   (D) thought to be

2. (A) enough hungry   (B) hungry enough

  (C) as hungry as   (D) too hungry

3. (A) serving   (B) served

  (C) to serve them   (D) they served

4. (A) enables   (B) motivates

  (C) has   (D) makes

5. (A) where it   (B) where

  (C) as   (D) which

TEST 18 詳解

There is no accounting for tastes. One person's meat may be another's poison. For example, insects, candied or fried, are <u>thought to be</u> mouth-watering foods in some

1
parts of the world, while in other regions roasted mice are a delicacy.

人的喜好是無法解釋的。你口中的肉，可能是其他人的毒藥。例如，用糖醃漬或是油炸昆蟲，在世界上某些地區，被認爲是令人垂涎三尺的食物，而有些地區則是把烤老鼠當作佳餚。

** *There is no V-ing* ～是不可能的（ = *It is impossible to V.*）
 ***account for* 說明　 taste〔test〕*n.* 喜好**
 ***There is no accounting for tastes.* 【諺】人各有所好。**
 meat〔mit〕*n.* 肉　 poison〔'pɔɪzn̩〕*n.* 毒藥
 One person's meat may be another's poison.
 　 【諺】對甲是肉，對乙是毒；人各有所好。
 insect〔'ɪnsɛkt〕*n.* 昆蟲
 candy〔'kændɪ〕*v.* 用糖醃漬　 fry〔fraɪ〕*v.* 油炸
 mouth-watering〔'maʊθ‚wɔtərɪŋ〕*adj.* 令人垂涎的
 region〔'ridʒən〕*n.* 地區　 roast〔rost〕*v.* 烤
 mice〔maɪs〕*n. pl.* 老鼠
 delicacy〔'dɛləkəsɪ〕*n.* 美食；佳餚

1. (**D**) 依句意，選 (D) *be thought to be*「被認爲是」。而 (A) 須改爲 considered to be，(B) 須改爲 looked upon as，(C) 須改爲 thought of as 才能選。

Likewise, Americans may say that they are "<u>hungry enough</u>

2

to eat a horse," but if <u>served</u> horsemeat, which is actually

3

eaten in some areas of France, they would never try it.

同樣地，美國人說：「我餓得可以吃下一隻馬，」但是如果把馬
肉端到他們面前，美國人絕不會嚐試，然而在法國的某些地方還
眞的會吃馬肉。

    ** likewise〔'laɪk,waɪz〕*adv.* 同樣地

        horsemeat〔'hɔrs'mit〕*n.* 馬肉

        actually〔'æktʃʊəlɪ〕*adv.* 實際上

  2. (**B**) enough 須放在所修飾的形容詞之後，又 enough to
       表「足以~」，故選 (B) *hungry enough*。

  3. (**B**) 原句爲：…but if *they are served* horsemeat…，
       副詞子句中，句意很明顯，主詞和 be 動詞可同時省略，
       故選 (B) *served*。
       serve〔sɝv〕*v.* 供應

    In fact, a mixture of some factors <u>motivates</u> us to

4

choose certain foods. The geography of the country has an

important role in food selection. Millet is a type of grain

eaten in Africa, <u>where it</u> is plentiful, but in other places it

5

is used as birdseed.

　　事實上，促使我們選擇某些食物的原因有很多。國家的地理環境在食物選擇上扮演重要的角色。小米在非洲產量豐富，所以是食用的穀物之一，但在其他地方卻被當成鳥飼料。

> ** ***in fact*** 事實上　　　mixture〔ˈmɪkstʃɚ〕*n.* 混合
> factor〔ˈfæktɚ〕*n.* 因素
> geography〔dʒɪˈɑɡrəfɪ〕*n.* 地理；地形
> selection〔səˈlɛkʃən〕*n.* 選擇
> millet〔ˈmɪlɪt〕*n.* 小米；粟
> grain〔gren〕*n.* 穀物　　　Africa〔ˈæfrɪkə〕*n.* 非洲
> plentiful〔ˈplɛntɪfəl〕*adj.* 豐富的
> birdseed〔ˈbɝdˌsid〕*n.* 鳥食

4. (**B**)　依句意，選 (B) ***motivates***。

　　motivate〔ˈmotəˌvet〕*v.* 促使
　　而 (A) enable「使能夠」，不合句意；而 (C) has「叫」，(D) make「使」，為使役動詞，接受詞後，須接原形動詞，在此用法不合。

5. (**A**)　表地點，關係副詞用 where，又 where 引導的形容詞子句中，須有主詞，故選 (A) ***where it***。

┌─── 【劉毅老師的話】 ───
│　　　多做克漏字測驗，熟能生巧，
│　克漏字滿分就不再是夢想。
└────────────────

TEST 19

Read the following passage and choose the best answer for each blank from the choices below.

One way to improve our relationships with others is to develop a greater sense of empathy. This involves emotionally ___1___ ourselves in the place of another. To do so, we have to be aware of our own feelings first. ___2___, we should recognize and acknowledge our feelings rather than belittle or ignore their existence. Allowing ourselves to experience feelings ___3___ us to maintain emotional balance.

1. (A) put   (B) puts
   (C) to put   (D) putting

2. (A) Similarly   (B) That is
   (C) Instead   (D) On the other hand

3. (A) enables   (B) affects
   (C) determine   (D) ignore

This in turn raises our level of sensitivity, which

___4___ our ability to notice others' feelings and to

feel something ourselves. In the process of getting

to know others on such a level, we find all humans

have similar emotional needs. And that's why we

can empathize with others and handle things in a

more ___5___ way.

【成功高中】

4. (A) points out   (B) plays a part in
   (C) deals with   (D) works toward

5. (A) irrational   (B) critical
   (C) constructive   (D) negative

TEST 19 詳解

One way to improve our relationships with others is to develop a greater sense of empathy. This involves emotionally <u>putting</u> ourselves in the place of another. To do so, we have
　　　1
to be aware of our own feelings first. <u>That is</u>, we should
　　　　　　　　　　　　　　　　　　　　2
recognize and acknowledge our feelings rather than belittle or ignore their existence.

有一種改善人際關係的方法，那就是要多培養同理心。這需要在情感上讓自己設身處地爲他人著想。要這麼做，就必須先了解自己的情緒。也就是說，我們應該要認清並承認自己的情感，而不是輕視或忽略它們的存在。

　　** improve〔ɪm'pruv〕v. 改善　　sense〔sɛns〕n. 感覺
　　　empathy〔'ɛmpəθɪ〕n. 同理心；感同身受
　　　emotionally〔ɪ'moʃənḷɪ〕adv. 在情緒上
　　　be aware of 知道；察覺到
　　　recognize〔'rɛkəg͵naɪz〕v. 認清
　　　acknowledge〔ək'nɑlɪdʒ〕v. 承認
　　　rather than 而不是　　belittle〔bɪ'lɪtḷ〕v. 輕視
　　　ignore〔ɪg'nor〕v. 忽視
　　　existence〔ɪg'zɪstəns〕n. 存在

1. (**D**)　involves（需要）爲及物動詞，其後須接名詞或動名詞爲
　　　　　　受詞，故選 (D) ***putting***。
　　　　　put *oneself* ***in the place of another*** 使自己處在別人
　　　　　的地位；設身處地

2. (**B**) 依句意，選 (B) ***That is*** 「也就是說」。而 (A) similarly
   〔'sɪmələˌlɪ 〕 *adv.* 同樣地，(C) instead「取而代之」，
   (D) on the other hand「另一方面」，則不合句意。

Allowing ourselves to experience feelings <u>enables</u> us to
                                                    3
maintain emotional balance. This in turn raises our level of
sensitivity, which <u>plays a part in</u> our ability to notice others'
                            4
feelings and to feel something ourselves.

讓自己體驗情感，能使我們能夠保持情緒上的平靜。這樣必然就能
提高我們的敏感度，而這敏銳度的作用是讓我們能注意到他人情感，
以及自己能有某種感受。

> ** experience 〔 ɪk'spɪrɪəns 〕 *v.* 經歷；體驗
> maintain 〔 men'ten 〕 *v.* 保持；維持
> emotional 〔 ɪ'moʃənl̩ 〕 *adj.* 情緒的
> balance 〔'bæləns 〕 *n.* 平衡；平靜
> ***in turn*** 依序地；必然也
> sensitivity 〔ˌsɛnsə'tɪvətɪ 〕 *n.* 靈敏（度）
> notice 〔'notɪs 〕 *v.* 注意到

3. (**A**) 依句意，「使」我們「能夠」維持情緒上的平靜，選 (A)
   enables。而 (B) affect 〔 ə'fɛkt 〕 *v.* 影響，(C) determine
   〔 dɪ't3mɪn 〕 *v.* 決定，(D) ignore 〔 ɪg'nor 〕 *v.* 忽視，則不
   合句意。

4. (**B**) 依句意，選 (B) ***plays a part in***「在…扮演一個角色；在…
起作用」。而 (A) point out「指出」，(C) deal with
「應付；處理」，(D) work toward「努力達到；設法獲
得」，均不合句意。

In the process of getting to know others on such a level, we
find all humans have similar emotional needs. And that's
why we can empathize with others and handle things in a
more <u>constructive</u> way.
　　　　　 5
在這種程度上，漸漸了解他人的過程中，我們會發現，所有人都有
類似的情感需求。這也就是為什麼我們會和別人有同感，並且能以
較具有建設性的方法來處理事情。

    ** process〔'prɑsɛs〕*n.* 過程　　　***get to V.*** 得以～
    empathize〔'ɛmpə,θaɪz〕*v.* 有同理心；有同感
    handle〔'hændḷ〕*v.* 處理

5. (**C**) (A) irrational〔ɪ'ræʃənḷ〕*adj.* 不理性的；不合理的
    (B) critical〔'krɪtɪkḷ〕*adj.* 愛批評的；吹毛求疵的
    (C) ***constructive***〔kən'strʌktɪv〕*adj.* 有建設性的
    (D) negative〔'nɛgətɪv〕*adj.* 負面的

TEST 20

*Read the following passage and choose the best answer for each
blank from the choices below.*

Most Americans prefer to keep a distance

between church and state. Students are not ___1___

to pray in schools and one must be careful not to

mix politics with religion. ___2___ this distinct

separation, Americans are quick to call upon God's

help and blessings in many situations.

The most obvious is the common blessing one

receives when ___3___ the common cold and a fit

of sneezing. When simple sniffles become full-blown

sneezes, it is ___4___ in America to say, "God bless

you" to the person after he or she sneezes.

The basis of this custom is the belief that a demon lies within the sick person. ___5___ rid of the demon, the sick person has to sneeze. However, sneezing could also expel the soul from the body. So the name of God is called as a prayer to protect him.

【師大附中】

1. (A) admitted (B) required
   (C) persuaded (D) restrained

2. (A) In addition to (B) As a result of
   (C) Despite (D) In case

3. (A) associated with (B) infecting with
   (C) suffering from (D) suffered from

4. (A) spontaneous (B) customary
   (C) practical (D) intelligent

5. (A) Getting (B) To get
   (C) Having gotten (D) As soon as he gets

TEST 20 詳解

Most Americans prefer to keep a distance between church and state. Students are not <u>required</u> to pray in schools and one
1
must be careful not to mix politics with religion. <u>Despite</u> this
2
distinct separation, Americans are quick to call upon God's help and blessings in many situations.

大部分的美國人比較喜歡將教會跟國家劃清界線。學生在學校不需要禱告，而且必須要小心，不要把政治跟宗教混在一起。儘管區隔如此明顯，但美國人在許多情況中，常會急切地要求上帝的幫助跟祝福。

** prefer〔prɪˋfɝ〕*v.* 較喜愛；偏好
keep a distance between A ***and*** B 將 A 與 B 劃清界線
church〔tʃɝtʃ〕*n.* 教會　　state〔stet〕*n.* 國家
pray〔pre〕*v.* 祈禱　　***mix*** A ***with*** B 將 A 與 B 混在一起
politics〔ˋpɑləˏtɪks〕*n.* 政治（學）
religion〔rɪˋlɪdʒən〕*n.* 宗教
distinct〔dɪˋstɪŋkt〕*adj.* 不同的；清楚的
separation〔ˏsɛpəˋreʃən〕*n.* 分別；分離
call upon 要求　　blessing〔ˋblɛsɪŋ〕*n.* 神恩；祝福
situation〔ˏsɪtʃʊˋeʃən〕*n.* 情況

1. (**B**) 依句意，選 (B) ***be required to***「必須」。而 (A) admit〔ədˋmɪt〕*v.* 准許進入，(C) persuade〔pɚˋswed〕*v.* 說服，(D) restrain〔rɪˋstren〕*v.* 克制；限制，均不合句意。

2. (**C**)　依句意，選 (C) *despite*「儘管」。而 (A) in addition to「除了…之外（還有）」，(B) as a result of「因為；由於」，(D) in case「以防萬一」，均不合句意。

The most obvious is the common blessing one receives when <u>suffering from</u> the common cold and a fit of sneezing.
　　　　　　　　3
When simple sniffles become full-blown sneezes, it is <u>customary</u>
　　　　　　　　　　　　　　　　　　　　　　　　　　　4
in America to say, "God bless you" to the person after he or she sneezes.

　　最明顯的，就是當有人罹患普通感冒，並連續打噴嚏時，常聽到的祝福話語。當單純的鼻塞變成完全喘不過氣來的噴嚏時，美國人習慣在對方打完噴嚏後，對他或她說：「願上帝祝福你。」

　　** obvious〔'abvɪəs〕*adj.* 明顯的
　　　common〔'kamən〕*adj.* 常見的；一般的
　　　receive〔rɪ'siv〕*v.* 接到；得到　　　cold〔kold〕*n.* 感冒
　　　fit〔fɪt〕*n.* 一陣　　　sneeze〔sniz〕*v.* 打噴嚏　*n.* 噴嚏
　　　sniffle〔'snɪfḷ〕*n.* 鼻塞；鼻炎
　　　full-blown〔'fʊl'blon〕*adj.* 完全喘不過氣來的
　　　God bless you. 願上帝祝福你。

3. (**C**)　本句是由…when he was suffering from the common cold…簡化而來，因為句意很明確，副詞子句中的主詞和 be 動詞（he was）可同時省略，故選 (C) *suffering from*「罹患」。而 (A) be associated with「與～有關」，不合句意；(B) 須改為 infected with「感染到～」才能選。

4. (**B**)　(A) spontaneous〔spɑn'tenɪəs〕*adj.* 自發性的

(B) ***customary***〔'kʌstəm,ɛrɪ〕*adj.* 習慣性的；慣例的

(C) practical〔'præktɪkḷ〕*adj.* 實際的

(D) intelligent〔ɪn'tɛlədʒənt〕*adj.* 聰明的

The basis of this custom is the belief that a demon lies within the sick person. <u>To get</u> rid of the demon, the sick
5
person has to sneeze. However, sneezing could also expel the soul from the body. So the name of God is called as a prayer to protect him.

這項習俗是基於人們相信魔鬼存在於病人體內。為了擺脫魔鬼，病人必須要打噴嚏。然而，打噴嚏也可能會把靈魂趕出體外。所以要呼喊上帝之名作為祈禱文，來保護病人。

** basis〔'besɪs〕*n.* 基本原則

custom〔'kʌstəm〕*n.* 習俗；慣例

belief〔bɪ'lif〕*n.* 信念；信仰；相信

demon〔'dimən〕*n.* 魔鬼　　***lie within*** 在…之內

expel〔ɪk'spɛl〕*v.* 驅逐；排出　　soul〔sol〕*n.* 靈魂

prayer〔prɛr〕*n.* 祈禱文　　protect〔prə'tɛkt〕*v.* 保護；保佑

5. (**B**)　表「目的」須用不定詞，故選 (B) ***to get rid of***「為了除去；為了擺脫」。

TEST 21

Read the following passage and choose the best answer for each blank from the choices below.

Believe it or not, you can now read entire novels on your cell phone. The novels are sent in short installments as text messages. ___1___ are the biggest audience, but the trend is slowly ___2___ with older readers, too.

Because phones can receive only small amounts of text, each installment ___3___ short. A few writers even make their novels interactive.

1. (A) Teenagers   (B) Managers
    (C) The elderly   (D) Senior citizens

2. (A) adding up   (B) coming down
    (C) catching on   (D) dying out

3. (A) must be   (B) can be
    (C) has been   (D) will have been

Readers send their comments to the writer after each new installment of a novel, and the writer ___4___ users' suggestions to create new plot twists. One such novel, *Deep Love*, was later published as a conventional book in Japan. It became a bestseller and was even made into a movie.

Book lovers may wonder if the tiny cell phone screen will make reading difficult. But ___5___ the novels' fans, the screens are much easier to read than you might imagine. So next time you need something to pass the time, try reading a novel on your phone!【師大附中】

4. (A) forms   (B) adopts
   (C) refuses   (D) expresses

5. (A) based on   (B) in addition to
   (C) except for   (D) according to

TEST 21 詳解

Believe it or not, you can now read entire novels on your cell phone. The novels are sent in short installments as text messages. Teenagers are the biggest audience, but the trend

<u>1</u>

is slowly catching on with older readers, too.

<u>2</u>

信不信由你，現在你能在手機上讀到整本小說。小說是以簡訊，用短篇連載的方式傳送。青少年是最主要的觀眾，但是這股潮流也慢慢地受到年長讀者的歡迎。

** ***believe it or not*** 信不信由你

entire〔ɪn'taɪr〕*adj.* 完整的

novel〔'nɑvḷ〕*n.* 小說　　***cell phone*** 手機

installment〔ɪn'stɔlmənt〕*n.* (連載刊物的)一回；

一個章節

text〔tɛkst〕*n.* 文句　　***text message*** 簡訊

audience〔'ɔdɪəns〕*n.* 觀眾

trend〔trɛnd〕*n.* 潮流

1. (**A**)　由句尾的 older readers (較年長的讀者)可知，空格應填年輕人，故選 (A) ***Teenagers***。

teenager〔'tin,edʒɚ〕*n.* 青少年

而 (B) manager「經理」，(C) the elderly「老人」，

(D) senior citizen「老人」，均不合句意。

elderly〔'ɛldɚlɪ〕*adj.* 年長的

senior〔'sinjɚ〕*adj.* 資深的；年長的

citizen〔'sɪtəzn̩〕*n.* 公民

2. (**C**) 依句意，選 (C) *catching on*「受歡迎」。

　　catch on with 受～歡迎

　　而 (A) add up「合計」，(B) come down with「因～而病倒」，(D) die out「逐漸消失；滅絕」，則不合句意。

Because phones can receive only small amounts of text, each installment <u>must be</u> short.　A few writers even make their
　　　　　　　　　　　3
novels interactive.　Readers send their comments to the writer after each new installment of a novel, and the writer <u>adopts</u>
　　　　　　　　　　　　　　　　　　　　　　　4
users' suggestions to create new plot twists.　One such novel, *Deep Love*, was later published as a conventional book in Japan.　It became a bestseller and was even made into a movie.

　　因為手機只能接收少量的內容，所以每一回的份量必須簡短。有些作者甚至讓他們的小說變得有互動性。讀者每看完新的一回後，就會回傳評論給小說的作者，然後作者會採用手機用戶的意見，創造新的劇情進展。在日本，有一本這樣的互動性的小說，名叫「深沉的愛」，之後出版成傳統書籍。它成為暢銷書，甚至被拍成電影。

　　** interactive〔͵ɪntə'æktɪv〕*adj.* 互相影響的；交互作用的

　　comment〔'kɑmɛnt〕*n.* 評論　　user〔'juzɚ〕*n.* 使用者；用戶

　　suggestion〔səg'dʒɛstʃən〕*n.* 建議　　create〔krɪ'et〕*v.* 創造

　　plot〔plɑt〕*n.* 情節　　twist〔twɪst〕*n.* 意外進展

　　Deep Love 深沉的愛【日本年度暢銷小說，描寫援交少女重生的故事，原本在手機網站提供下載而受到青少女歡迎，出版後銷售量近三百萬冊】　　publish〔'pʌblɪʃ〕*v.* 出版

　　conventional〔kən'vɛnʃən!〕*adj.* 傳統的

　　bestseller〔'bɛst'sɛlɚ〕*n.* 暢銷書

　　be made into 被製成；被拍成

3. (**A**) 依句意,每一回都「必須」要很短,故選 (A) *must be*。

4. (**B**) (A) form〔fɔrm〕*v.* 形成
　　　　　(B) *adopt*〔ə'dɑpt〕*v.* 採用
　　　　　(C) refuse〔rɪ'fjuz〕*v.* 拒絕
　　　　　(D) express〔ɪk'sprɛs〕*v.* 表達

　　Book lovers may wonder if the tiny cell phone screen will make reading difficult. But <u>according to</u> the novels' fans, the
　　　　　　　　　　　　　　　　　　　5
screens are much easier to read than you might imagine. So next time you need something to pass the time, try reading a novel on your phone!

　　愛讀書的人可能會想知道,小小的手機螢幕,是不是會使閱讀變得很困難。但根據小說迷的說法,螢幕其實比你想像的更容易閱讀。所以下次如果你需要某些東西來打發時間的話,試試看在你的手機上看小說吧!

　　** *book lover* 愛書人　　wonder〔'wʌndɚ〕*v.* 想知道
　　　　tiny〔'taɪnɪ〕*adj.* 極小的　　screen〔skrin〕*n.* 螢幕
　　　　fan〔fæn〕*n.*(書、電影的)迷
　　　　imagine〔ɪ'mædʒɪn〕*v.* 想像
　　　　pass the time 打發時間

5. (**D**) 「根據」小說迷「的說法」,選 (D) *according to*。而 (A) based on「根據」,其後不可直接接「人」,須接「某人的說法」,故用法不合;而 (B) in addition to「除了~之外(還有)」,(C) except for「除了~之外」,則不合句意。

TEST 22

*Read the following passage and choose the best answer for each
blank from the choices below.*

    Several boys and girls got on the bus and dreamed

of the golden beaches and sea tides in Florida. A

man sat in front of them, dressed in a plain, ill-fitting

suit, never moving, his dusty face ___1___ his age.

He chewed the inside of his lip a lot, ___2___ into

some personal cocoon of silence. Finally, the man

told his story. He said that he had been in jail for the

past four years, and ___3___ he was going home.

He had written his wife that if she would forgive him,

she should put a yellow handkerchief on the old oak

tree near their home. Then, suddenly, all the young

people were up out of their seats, screaming and

shouting, and crying, doing small dances of exultation.

The man sat there ___4___, looking at the oak tree,

which ___5___ hundreds of yellow handkerchiefs.

He rose excitedly from his seat and made his way

to the front of the bus to go home. 【中正高中】

1. (A) masking   (B) mask
   (C) masks   (D) to mask

2. (A) freeze   (B) freezing
   (C) froze   (D) frozen

3. (A) which   (B) how
   (C) that   (D) whether

4. (A) was stunned   (B) stunning
   (C) to stun   (D) stunned

5. (A) covered   (B) was covered with
   (C) was covering   (D) covered with

TEST 22 詳解

Several boys and girls got on the bus and dreamed of the golden beaches and sea tides in Florida. A man sat in front of them, dressed in a plain, ill-fitting suit, never moving, his dusty face <u>masking</u> his age. He chewed the inside of his lip a lot,
  1
<u>frozen</u> into some personal cocoon of silence.
  2

有幾個男孩跟女孩搭上了公車，幻想著佛羅里達的金色海灘跟浪潮。有個男人坐在他們前面，穿著普通又不合身的西裝，一動也不動，他灰暗的臉龐讓人看不出他幾歲。他苦惱地緊咬著內嘴唇，好像凍結在自己安靜的繭裡。

> ** ***dream of*** 夢想；幻想　　tide〔taɪd〕*n.* 潮水
> Florida〔'flɔrədə〕*n.* 佛羅里達州【美國東南端的一州】
> plain〔plen〕*adj.* 不講究的；樸素的
> ill-fitting〔'ɪl'fɪtɪŋ〕*adj.* 不合身的
> suit〔sut〕*n.* 西裝　　dusty〔'dʌstɪ〕*adj.* 佈滿灰塵的
> chew〔tʃu〕*v.* 咬；咀嚼
> inside〔'ɪn'saɪd〕*n.* 內部；裡面　　lip〔lɪp〕*n.* 嘴唇
> ***chew*** *one's* ***lips*** 忍住（怒氣、苦惱等）而咬嘴唇（= *bite one's lips*）　　*a lot* 常常　　cocoon〔kə'kun〕*n.* 繭
> silence〔'saɪləns〕*n.* 沉默；安靜

1. (**A**)　本句的主要動詞是 sat，其後都未出現連接詞，故後面的動詞均以分詞型態呈現，如 dressed in（穿著～），故空格也須填分詞，且依句意為主動，須用現在分詞，故選 (A) ***masking***。　　mask〔mæsk〕*v.* 隱藏；掩飾

2. (**D**)　原句為 He chewed the inside of his lip a lot, and was
　　　frozen into…，對等連接詞 and 省略，was 須改為現在分
　　　詞 being，又 being 也可省略，故選 (D) *frozen*。
　　　freeze〔friz〕*v.* 使凍結；使呆住；使一動也不動

Finally, the man told his story. He said that he had been in jail
for the past four years, and that he was going home. He had
　　　　　　　　　　　　　　　3
written his wife that if she would forgive him, she should put
a yellow handkerchief on the old oak tree near their home.
最後，這個男人開始講自己的故事。他說他過去四年都待在監獄裡，
現在正要回家。他寫信給妻子說，如果她肯原諒他的話，就在他們家
附近的老橡樹上綁一條黃色手帕。

　　　** jail〔dʒel〕*n.* 監獄　　*write sb.* 寫信給某人
　　　　　forgive〔fəˈgɪv〕*v.* 原諒
　　　　　handkerchief〔ˈhæŋkətʃɪf〕*n.* 手帕　　oak〔ok〕*n.* 橡樹

3. (**C**)　對等連接詞 and 連接兩個 that 引導的名詞子句，且第二個
　　　that 不可省略，故選 (C)。

Then, suddenly, all the young people were up out of their seats,
screaming and shouting, and crying, doing small dances of
exultation. The man sat there stunned, looking at the oak tree,
　　　　　　　　　　　　　　　　　　　4
which was covered with hundreds of yellow handkerchiefs.
　　　　5
He rose excitedly from his seat and made his way to the front
of the bus to go home.

然後，突然間，所有的年輕人都從椅子上站起來，大聲尖叫、大喊，因狂喜而跳了一小段舞。那男人呆坐在那裡，看著橡樹上綁滿數百條黃色手帕。他很興奮地從位子上站起來，走到公車前面，然後回家。

** suddenly〔'sʌdn̩lɪ〕*adv.* 突然地

up〔ʌp〕*adv.* 起來　　　scream〔skrim〕*v.* 尖叫

shout〔ʃaʊt〕*v.* 喊叫

do a small dance 跳一小段舞（ = *do a short dance*）

exultation〔͵ɛgzʌl'teʃən〕*n.* 狂喜

hundreds of 數百個　　　rise〔raɪz〕*v.* 起立

excitedly〔ɪk'saɪtɪdlɪ〕*adv.* 興奮地

make one's ***way*** 前進；去

4. (**D**) 動詞 sit, stand, lie 後面可接形容詞或分詞，做主詞補語，如 sit still（坐著不動）、stand still（站著不動）、lie still（躺著不動）等，故空格應填分詞，做形容詞用，且依句意，選 (D) ***stunned***〔stʌnd〕*adj.*（人）目瞪口呆的。而 (B) stunning「使人目瞪口呆的」，用於形容事物，在此不合。

5. (**B**) which 引導形容詞子句，在子句中，which 做主詞，故空格應填動詞，且依句意為被動語態，故選 (B) ***was covered with***「被～覆蓋；佈滿了～」。

TEST 23

Read the following passage and choose the best answer for each
blank from the choices below.

Many young people are crazy about such

exciting sports as snowboarding, bungee jumping,

and scooter riding because they are daring and

somewhat trendy. However, it is nothing ___1___

recklessness if they try these sports with ___2___

or no preparation. If you want to try one of these

sports, first of all, you must have the right equipment

because ___3___ will help you enjoy yourself safely.

1. (A) like   (B) than
   (C) for   (D) but

2. (A) many   (B) an amount
   (C) little   (D) a few

3. (A) what   (B) they
   (C) it   (D) some

You can watch other people ___4___ these activities first and determine what safety precautions are being used. Moreover, you should never do these dangerous sports alone. Someone should be by your side when you dive, hang glide, or bungee jump to make sure you are safe or to help ___5___ an emergency. "Safety first" may be the guideline for survival, but ironically, the reason some of these sports are so attractive and interesting is that they are life-threatening. 【中正高中】

4. (A) do   (B) to do
   (C) been done   (D) having to do

5. (A) in   (B) at
   (C) on   (D) with

TEST 23 詳解

Many young people are crazy about such exciting sports as snowboarding, bungee jumping, and scooter riding because they are daring and somewhat trendy. However, it is nothing <u>but</u> recklessness if they try these
                                                           1
sports with <u>little</u> or no preparation.
            2

很多年輕人非常熱衷於刺激的運動，像是玩滑雪板、高空彈跳，還有騎機車，因為他們膽子很大，又有點喜歡追求流行。然而，如果他們嘗試這些運動，但卻很少或沒有做準備，那就太魯莽了。

** ***be crazy about*** 熱衷於
　　exciting (ɪk'saɪtɪŋ) *adj.* 刺激的
　　snowboard ('sno,bord) *v.* 玩滑雪板　　*n.* 滑雪板
　　bungee jump ('bʌndʒi,dʒʌmp) *v.* 玩高空彈跳　　*n.* 高空彈跳
　　scooter ('skutɚ) *n.* 機車 (指有腳踏板的機車)
　　scooter riding 騎機車
　　daring ('dɛrɪŋ) *adj.* 勇敢的；大膽的
　　somewhat ('sʌm,hwɑt) *adv.* 有點
　　trendy ('trɛndɪ) *adj.* 趕時髦的；追求流行的
　　recklessness ('rɛklɪsnɪs) *n.* 魯莽
　　preparation (,prɛpə'reʃən) *n.* 準備

1. (**D**) ***nothing but*** 只是 (= *only*)

2. (**C**) 依句意，選 (C) ***little***「很少」。

If you want to try one of these sports, first of all, you must have the right equipment because <u>it</u> will help you enjoy
    3
yourself safely. You can watch other people <u>do</u> these
    4
activities first and determine what safety precautions are being used.

如果想嘗試這些運動的其中一種，首先就必須要有適當的裝備，這樣才能安全地玩樂。你可以先看別人怎麼做這些活動，然後決定要使用哪些安全措施。

> ** **_first of all_** 首先　　equipment 〔 ɪˈkwɪpmənt 〕 *n.* 裝備
> **_enjoy_** *oneself* 玩得愉快　　activity 〔 ækˈtɪvətɪ 〕 *n.* 活動
> determine 〔 dɪˈtɝmɪn 〕 *v.* 決定
> precaution 〔 prɪˈkɔʃən 〕 *n.* 預防措施
> **_safety precaution_** 安全措施

3. (**C**)　依句意，「它」會幫助你安全地玩樂，選 (C) **_it_** 。

4. (**A**)　watch 是感官動詞，接受詞後，須接原形動詞或現在
 　　　　分詞表主動，故選 (A) **_do_** 。

Moreover, you should never do these dangerous sports alone. Someone should be by your side when you dive, hang glide, or bungee jump to make sure you are safe or to help <u>in</u> an emergency. "Safety first" may be the
    5
guideline for survival, but ironically, the reason some of these sports are so attractive and interesting is that they are life-threatening.

此外，你絕對不該單獨做這些危險的運動。在你跳傘、玩滑翔翼，
或是高空彈跳的時候，身邊應該要有其他人，確保你安全無虞，或
是當緊急情況發生時，可以伸出援手。「安全第一」可能是存活的
準則，但諷刺的是，某些運動會如此吸引人，而且又有趣的原因，
就是因為它們會危及生命。

> ** alone〔ə'lon〕*adv.* 獨自地
> ***by one's side*** 在某人身旁
> dive〔daɪv〕*v.* 跳水；跳傘
> hang〔hæŋ〕*v.* 垂下　　glide〔glaɪd〕*v.* 滑動
> ***hang glide*** 滑翔翼運動　　***make sure*** 確認
> emergency〔ɪ'mɝdʒənsɪ〕*n.* 緊急情況
> ***safety first*** 安全第一
> guideline〔'gaɪd‚laɪn〕*n.* 指導方針；準則
> survival〔sə'vaɪv!〕*n.* 生存；生還
> ironically〔aɪ'rɑnɪk!ɪ〕*adv.* 諷刺的是
> attractive〔ə'træktɪv〕*adj.* 吸引人的
> life-threatening〔'laɪf'θrɛtṇɪŋ〕*adj.* 可能導致生命危險的；
>   危及生命的

5. (**A**)　「在」緊急情況，介系詞用 ***in***，故選 (A)。

【劉毅老師的話】

　　平常練習做題目時，要養成計
時的習慣，訓練自己的速度，這樣
考試時才不會緊張。

TEST 24

Read the following passage and choose the best answer for each blank from the choices below.

High school students in Taiwan have a heavy load of schoolwork. But we still spare time to do ___1___ activities. Take myself for example. I am on the school basketball team, and this year our team won the championship in the citywide ___2___. This was really something. All of our hard work ___3___. In addition to playing basketball, I also like to mingle with people. I enjoy ___4___ with my friends. But I am not allowed to date yet, not even a double date. My parents are very conservative. How I wish they ___5___ more liberal. Next week is our first monthly exam. A dark cloud of stress is looming, but I hope to pass the exam ___6___. I am keeping my fingers crossed. 【師大附中】

1. (A) extraterrestrial   (B) territorial
   (C) extracurricular   (D) circular

2. (A) meet   (B) gang
   (C) tournament   (D) appointment

3. (A) deserves   (B) paid off
   (C) feeds   (D) sacrifices

4. (A) sticking to   (B) mapping out
   (C) hanging out   (D) piling up

5. (A) were   (B) will be
   (C) are   (D) should have been

6. (A) as a matter of urgency
   (B) in a low tone
   (C) with flying colors
   (D) in disguise

TEST 24 詳解

High school students in Taiwan have a heavy load of schoolwork. But we still spare time to do <u>extracurricular</u> activities.
                                         1

台灣的高中生課業負擔很重。但我們還是會騰出時間做課外活動。

** load〔lod〕*n.* 重擔　　schoolwork〔'skul,wɜk〕*n.* 功課
spare〔spɛr〕*v.* 騰出 (時間)
activity〔æk'tɪvətɪ〕*n.* 活動

1. (**C**) 依句意，騰出時間從事「課外」活動，選 (C)
   extracurricular〔,ɛkstrəkə'rɪkjələ〕*adj.* 課外的。而
   (A) extraterrestrial〔,ɛkstrətə'rɛstrɪəl〕*adj.* 地球以外的
   n. 外星人，(B) territorial〔,tɛrə'torɪəl〕*adj.* 領土的，
   (D) circular〔'sɜkjələ〕*adj.* 圓形的，均不合句意。

Take myself for example. I am on the school basketball team, and this year our team won the championship in the citywide <u>tournament</u>. This was really something. All of
                          2
our hard work <u>paid off</u>.
                    3

以我自己爲例，我參加學校的籃球隊，而且今年我們球隊贏得全市的錦標賽冠軍。這眞是一件了不起的事，我們的辛苦都值得了。

　　** ***take sb. for example*** 以某人為例

　　championship〔'tʃæmpɪən,ʃɪp〕*n.* 冠軍

　　citywide〔'sɪtɪ,waɪd〕*adj.* 全市的

　　something〔'sʌmθɪŋ〕*pron.* 了不起的事

2. (**C**)　(A) meet〔mit〕*n.* 競賽大會；(運動)會

　　　　　(B) gang〔gæŋ〕*n.* 幫派

　　　　　(C) ***tournament***〔'tɝnəmənt〕*n.* 錦標賽

　　　　　(D) appointment〔ə'pɔɪntmənt〕*n.* 約會

3. (**B**)　(A) deserve〔dɪ'zɝv〕*v.* 應得(賞罰)

　　　　　(B) ***pay off*** 得到回報　　(C) feed〔fid〕*v.* 餵食

　　　　　(D) sacrifice〔'sækrə,faɪs〕*v.* 犧牲

In addition to playing basketball, I also like to mingle with
people. I enjoy <u>hanging out</u> with my friends. But I am not
　　　　　　　　　4
allowed to date yet, not even a double date. My parents are
very conservative. How I wish they <u>were</u> more liberal.
　　　　　　　　　　　　　　　5
除了打籃球之外，我還喜歡交朋友。我很喜歡跟朋友一起出去。
但我還不能約會，即使是雙對約會也不行。我的父母非常保守，
我真希望他們能更開明一點。

　　** ***in addition to*** 除了…之外(還有)

　　mingle〔'mɪŋgl̩〕*v.* 交往；交際　　***not…yet*** 尚未…

　　allow〔ə'laʊ〕*v.* 允許　　date〔det〕*v. n.* 約會

　　double date 雙對約會【兩對男女一起出去約會】

　　conservative〔kən'sɝvətɪv〕*adj.* 保守的

　　liberal〔'lɪbərəl〕*adj.* 開放的；開明的

4. (**C**) (A) stick to 堅持；遵守

(B) map out 詳盡地規劃

(C) ***hang out*** 閒蕩；鬼混

hang out with *sb.* 和某人出去

(D) pile up 堆積

5. (**A**) wish 表示不可能實現的願望，依句意，與現在事實相反，

須用過去式，且 be 動詞須用 ***were***，選 (A)。

Next week is our first monthly exam. A dark cloud of stress
is looming, but I hope to pass the exam with flying colors. I
am keeping my fingers crossed.
                                                                6

下星期就是我們第一次月考了。壓力的烏雲逐漸逼近，但我希望能得高
分通過考試。我會交叉手指以祈禱好運的。

** ***monthly exam*** 月考   cloud〔klaʊd〕*n.* 雲

dark cloud 烏雲   stress〔strɛs〕*n.* 壓力

loom〔lum〕*v.* (危險等) 迫近   pass〔pæs〕*v.* 通過

keep *one's* ***fingers crossed*** 手指交叉以祈求好運

【外國人習慣將中指與食指交叉，以祈求好運】

6. (**C**) (A) as a matter of urgency 是很迫切的事情

urgency〔'ɝdʒənsɪ〕*n.* 緊急；迫切

(B) in a low tone 用很低的音調

tone〔ton〕*n.* 音調

(C) ***with flying colors*** 出色地；成功地

(D) in disguise 偽裝的

TEST 25

Read the following passage and choose the best answer for each blank from the choices below.

Body language is a type of ___1___ signal. Any movement of any part of your body is a kind of nonverbal communication. ___2___, the way people use distance or space when they interact also ___3___ nonverbal messages. Generally speaking, there are two major types of body language. One is universal and ___4___ is not.

1. (A) spoken   (B) speaking
   (C) unspeaking   (D) unspoken

2. (A) Instead   (B) Though
   (C) Otherwise   (D) In addition

3. (A) to send   (B) sends
   (C) sending   (D) sent

4. (A) others   (B) another
   (C) other   (D) the other

The former, for example, includes smiling when we are happy or ___5___ our lips when we are angry. The latter might differ from culture to culture. Take the North American hand signal O.K. for example. It means money in Japan, ___6___ in South America it is considered a disgusting gesture. If people don't pay attention to this cultural difference, it can cause a lot of misunderstanding. Thus, when we learn another language, we must also know the differences in body language in different countries. 【陽明高中】

5. (A) tenses   (B) to tense

    (C) tensed   (D) tensing

6. (A) whereas   (B) hence

    (C) otherwise   (D) besides

TEST 25 詳解

Body language is a type of <u>unspoken</u> signal. Any
          1
movement of any part of your body is a kind of nonverbal
communication. <u>In addition</u>, the way people use distance or
       2
space when they interact also <u>sends</u> nonverbal messages.
            3

  肢體語言是一種無言的信號。你身體任何部位的任何動作,都是一種非語言的溝通。此外,人們與他人互動時,運用距離或空間的方式,也傳達了非語言的訊息。

  ** ***body language*** 肢體語言
   signal (ˈsɪɡn̩) *n.* 信號
   movement (ˈmuvmənt) *n.* 動作
   nonverbal (nɑnˈvɝbl̩) *adj.* 非語言的
   communication (kə͵mjunəˈkeʃən) *n.* 溝通
   nonverbal communication 非語言溝通
   distance (ˈdɪstəns) *n.* 距離 space (spes) *n.* 空間
   interact (͵ɪntɚˈækt) *v.* 互動

1. (**D**) 依句意,肢體語言是「無言的」信號,選 (D) ***unspoken***
   「無言的;不言而喻的」。而 (A) spoken「口頭的」,
   (B) speaking「說話的」,則不合句意;(C) 無 unspeaking
   這個字。

2. (**D**) 依句意,選 (D) ***In addition***「此外」。而 (A) instead「反而」,
   (B) though「雖然」,(C) otherwise (ˈʌðɚ͵waɪz) *adv.* 否則;
   要不然,則不合句意。

3. (**B**) the way 是主詞，people…interact 是省略關代 that 或
which 的形容詞子句，故空格應填動詞，且依句意為現在
式，故選 (B) *sends*。

Generally speaking, there are two major types of body
language. One is universal and <u>the other</u> is not. The former,
                                        4
for example, includes smiling when we are happy or <u>tensing</u>
                                                          5
our lips when we are angry. The latter might differ from
culture to culture.

一般說來，肢體語言有兩大類型。一種是普遍共用的，另一種不是。
例如，前者包括我們開心時的笑容，或生氣時緊閉的嘴唇。後者可能
隨文化而有所不同。

> ** *generally speaking* 一般說來
>
> major〔ˈmedʒɚ〕*adj.* 主要的
>
> universal〔͵junəˈvɝsḷ〕*adj.* 普遍的；共同的
>
> former〔ˈfɔrmɚ〕*adj.* 前者的　　include〔ɪnˈklud〕*v.* 包含
>
> lips〔lɪps〕*n. pl.* 嘴唇　　latter〔ˈlætɚ〕*adj.* 後者的
>
> *differ from* A *to* A　每個 A 都不同

4. (**D**) 只有兩者的情況，一個用 one，另一個用 *the other*，選 (D)。
而 (A) others「其他的人或物」，(B) another「（三者以上）
另一個」，(C) other「其他的」，均不合句意。

5. (**D**) or 為對等連接詞，前面是 smiling，所以空格應填動名詞，
故選 (D) *tensing*。
tense〔tɛns〕*v.* 使拉緊；使繃緊

Take the North American hand signal O.K. for example. It means
money in Japan, <u>whereas</u> in South America it is considered a
　　　　　　　　　　6
disgusting gesture.

以北美 "OK" 這個手勢爲例。在日本，它代表錢的意思，然而在南美
洲，它卻會被認爲是個噁心的手勢。

> ** *take…for example*　以…爲例
> mean〔min〕*v.* 意思是
> *South America* 南美洲　　consider〔kən'sɪdə〕*v.* 認爲
> disgusting〔dɪs'gʌstɪŋ〕*adj.* 噁心的
> gesture〔'dʒɛstʃə〕*n.* 手勢

6. (**A**)　表「對比」，選 (A) *whereas*〔hwɛr'æz〕*conj.*　然而
　　　(= *while*)。而 (B) hence〔hɛns〕*adv.* 因此，(C)
　　　otherwise「否則」，(D) besides「此外」，均不合句意。

If people don't pay attention to this cultural difference, it can
cause a lot of misunderstanding. Thus, when we learn another
language, we must also know the differences in body language
in different countries.

假如人們不去注意這樣的文化差異，就可能會造成許多誤會。因此，
當我們學習其他語言的時候，我們也必須了解在不同國家中，肢體語
言的差異。

> ** *pay attention to*　注意　　cultural〔'kʌltʃərəl〕*adj.* 文化的
> cause〔kɔz〕*v.* 引起；造成
> misunderstanding〔,mɪsʌndə'stændɪŋ〕*n.* 誤解；誤會
> thus〔ðʌs〕*adv.* 因此

TEST 26

Read the following passage and choose the best answer for each blank from the choices below.

A college student goes two nights without sleep to cram for exams and on the third day ___1___ a cold. A night-shift employee begins to work days and gets the flu. A patient who is awakened four times a night in the hospital begins to recover only after going home and getting a good night's sleep. Are these situations coincidental? Or do they show that sleep loss ___2___ illness? Despite intense interest, sleep researchers have been hard-pressed to show exactly how sleep ___3___ human health and disease. But new findings may shed light on the ultimate purpose of sleep and in particular on the interplay between sleep and the immune system.

Experiments suggest the immune system is somehow repaired or bolstered during sleep and that it, ___4___, helps regulate sleep. According to Canadian researcher Dr. Harvey Moldofsky, sleep ___5___ many purposes. Apparently, animals sleep to regulate body temperature, organize memories and strengthen the immune system.

【師大附中】

1. (A) gets over   (B) goes out of
   (C) comes down with   (D) comes under

2. (A) results from   (B) cures
   (C) prevents   (D) results in

3. (A) influences   (B) involves
   (C) manages   (D) effects

4. (A) for once   (B) in turn
   (C) after all   (D) at best

5. (A) does   (B) serves
   (C) frustrates   (D) makes

TEST 26 詳解

A college student goes two nights without sleep to cram for exams and on the third day <u>comes down with</u> a cold. A

1

night-shift employee begins to work days and gets the flu. A patient who is awakened four times a night in the hospital begins to recover only after going home and getting a good night's sleep. Are these situations coincidental? Or do they show that sleep loss <u>results in</u> illness?

2

有個大學生整整兩夜沒睡，為了考試臨時抱佛腳，第三天就感冒了。一位值夜班的員工開始在白天工作，然後就得了流行性感冒。一個在醫院每晚被吵醒四次的病人，只有在回家好好睡一覺後，才開始康復。這些情況都只是巧合嗎？或者是顯示睡眠不足會導致疾病？

** college〔ˈkɑlɪdʒ〕*n.* 大學　　***go without*** 沒有
　　cram〔kræm〕*v.* 死記硬背；臨時抱佛腳
　　night-shift〔ˈnaɪtˌʃɪft〕*adj.* 值夜班的
　　employee〔ˌɛmplɔɪˈi〕*n.* 員工　　days〔dez〕*adv.* 在白天
　　flu〔flu〕*n.* 流行性感冒 (= *influenza*)
　　patient〔ˈpeʃənt〕*n.* 病人　　awaken〔əˈwekən〕*v.* 吵醒
　　recover〔rɪˈkʌvɚ〕*v.* 康復　　***a good night's sleep*** 一夜好眠
　　situation〔ˌsɪtʃʊˈeʃən〕*n.* 情況
　　coincidental〔koˌɪnsəˈdɛntl̩〕*adj.* 巧合的
　　sleep loss 睡眠不足　　illness〔ˈɪlnɪs〕*n.* 疾病

1. (**C**)　(A) get over　克服；自～中恢復
　　　　　　(B) go out of　從～出去
　　　　　　(C) ***come down with***　因～而病倒；罹患
　　　　　　(D) come under　受到 (影響)；被～控制

2. (**D**) 依句意，選 (D) *result in*「導致；造成」。而 (A) result
from「起因於」，(B) cure〔kjʊr〕*v.* 治療，(C) prevent
「預防」，均不合句意。

Despite intense interest, sleep researchers have been hard-
pressed to show exactly how sleep <u>influences</u> human health
and disease.
                                3

儘管睡眠研究者有強烈的興趣，但卻很難確切地說明，睡眠如何影
響人類的健康與疾病。

  ** despite〔dɪ'spaɪt〕*prep.* 儘管   intense〔ɪn'tɛns〕*adj.* 強烈的
      hard-pressed〔'hɑrd'prɛst〕*adj.* 處於困境的；面臨困難的
      be hard-pressed to V. 很難~；不可能~   show〔ʃo〕*v.* 指出
      exactly〔ɪg'zæktlɪ〕*adv.* 確切地   disease〔dɪ'ziz〕*n.* 疾病

3. (**A**) (A) *influence*〔'ɪnfluəns〕*v.* 影響
        (B) involve〔ɪn'vɑlv〕*v.* 牽涉
        (C) manage〔'mænɪdʒ〕*v.* 管理；設法
        (D) effect〔ɪ'fɛkt〕*n.* 效果；影響

But new findings may shed light on the ultimate purpose of
sleep and in particular on the interplay between sleep and the
immune system. Experiments suggest the immune system is
somehow repaired or bolstered during sleep and that it, <u>in turn</u>,
helps regulate sleep.
                                        4

但新的研究結果，可能可以說明睡眠的最大效果，尤其是睡眠跟免疫
系統之間的交互作用。實驗顯示，睡覺時，免疫系統會以某種方式被
修復或強化，而且必然也有助於調節睡眠。

  ** findings〔'faɪndɪŋz〕*n. pl.* 研究的結果
      shed〔ʃɛd〕*v.* 發出（光、熱）   *shed light on* 照亮；闡明

ultimate〔ˈʌltəmɪt〕*adj.* 最終的；最大的
purpose〔ˈpɝpəs〕*n.* 目的；用途；效果
in particular 尤其；特別是
interplay〔ˈɪntɚˌple〕*n.* 交互作用
immune〔ɪˈmjun〕*adj.* 免疫的
experiment〔ɪkˈspɛrəmənt〕*n.* 實驗
suggest〔səgˈdʒɛst〕*v.* 暗示；顯示
somehow〔ˈsʌmˌhaʊ〕*adv.* 以某種方法
repair〔rɪˈpɛr〕*v.* 修理；恢復
bolster〔ˈbolstɚ〕*v.* 支撐；加強　　regulate〔ˈrɛgjəˌlet〕*v.* 調節

4.(**B**)　依句意，選 (B) ***in turn***「必然也」。而 (A) for once「至少一次」，(C) after all「畢竟」，(D) at best「充其量」，則不合句意。

According to Canadian researcher Dr. Harvey Moldofsky, sleep
<u>serves</u> many purposes. Apparently, animals sleep to regulate
　5
body temperature, organize memories and strengthen the
immune system.
根據加拿大研究人員哈維・莫多夫斯基博士的說法，睡眠有許多用途。
動物似乎是利用睡覺來調節體溫、組織記憶，並強化免疫系統。

** Canadian〔kəˈnedɪən〕*adj.* 加拿大的
apparently〔əˈpærəntlɪ〕*adv.* 表面上看來；似乎
organize〔ˈɔrgənˌaɪz〕*v.* 組織；使系統化
memory〔ˈmɛmərɪ〕*n.* 記憶（力）
strengthen〔ˈstrɛŋθən〕*v.* 強化

5.(**B**)　依句意，選 (B) ***serves many purposes***「有許多種用途」。
serve〔sɝv〕*v.* 符合（用途）；滿足（需要）
(C) frustrate〔ˈfrʌstret〕*v.* 使受挫

TEST 27

Read the following passage and choose the best answer for each blank from the choices below.

Although scientists now know a great deal about tornadoes, they are still unable to determine exactly when and where one will form. Tornadoes ___1___ all sizes, but ___2___ the major tornadoes ___2___ receive the most attention. The paths of these monster tornadoes are nearly impossible to predict. One might blow down a line of houses, and then suddenly lift up and leave one home intact before touching down again and ___3___ the rest of the line.

1. (A) come in   (B) come about
   (C) come with   (D) come along

2. (A) what is ; which   (B) not ; until
   (C) there is ; so   (D) it is ; that

3. (A) destroy   (B) destroyed
   (C) destroying   (D) to destroy

There are stories ____4___ death and destruction

____4___ strange scenes — chickens that still

survive but with all of their feathers gone, pieces

of straw stuck in trees. In a 1999 U.S. storm,

fierce winds from one tornado lifted a church into

the air and dropped it onto a house. In the same

storm, a baby was torn from its mother's arms

and later found ____5___ in a nearby tree. 【陽明高中】

4. (A) not only ; but also

   (B) not only of ; but also

   (C) not just of ; but of

   (D) not just ; but also of

5. (A) living   (B) lively

   (C) alive   (D) lived

TEST 27 詳解

    Although scientists now know a great deal about tornadoes, they are still unable to determine exactly when and where one will form. Tornadoes <u>come in</u> all sizes, but <u>it is</u> the major

1   2

tornadoes <u>that</u> receive the most attention.

2

    雖然科學家現在非常了解龍捲風，但卻仍然無法確定，在何時何地會形成龍捲風。龍捲風有各種不同的尺寸，但是較大的龍捲風才會比較受人注意。

> ** ***know about*** 知道   ***a great deal*** 很多
> tornado (tɔr'nedo) *n.* 龍捲風   ***unable to*** + ***V.*** 無法～
> determine (dɪ'tɝmɪn) *v.* 決定
> exactly (ɪg'zæktlɪ) *adv.* 確切地   form (fɔrm) *v.* 形成
> major ('medʒɚ) *adj.* 較大的   receive (rɪ'siv) *v.* 受到；接受
> attention (ə'tɛnʃən) *n.* 注意

1. (**A**) 依句意，選 (A) ***come in*** 「有（…尺寸、顏色、形狀等）」。

2. (**D**) 本句為強調句型，即：「It is + 強調部份 + that + 其餘部份」，故選 (D)。

    The paths of these monster tornadoes are nearly impossible to predict. One might blow down a line of houses, and then suddenly lift up and leave one home intact before touching down again and <u>destroying</u> the rest of the line.

3

這些巨大龍捲風的路徑幾乎無法預測。它可能會吹倒一整排房子，並且在再度接觸地面並摧毀其餘一整排房子之前，它會突然上升，留下一棟完整的房子。

    ** path〔pæθ〕*n.* 路徑；路線

       monster〔'mɑnstɚ〕*adj.* 巨大的

       nearly〔'nɪrlɪ〕*adv.* 幾乎   predict〔prɪ'dɪkt〕*v.* 預測

       blow down 吹倒   ***a line of*** 一整排

       suddenly〔'sʌdn̩lɪ〕*adv.* 突然地   lift〔lɪft〕*v.* 抬高；舉起

       lift up 舉起   leave〔liv〕*v.* 使處於（某種狀態）

       intact〔ɪn'tækt〕*adj.* 完整無缺的

       touch down 著陸；觸地   rest〔rɛst〕*n.* 其餘的人或物

3. (**C**) and 為對等連接詞，前面是動名詞片語 touching down，
        故空格須填動名詞，選 (C) ***destroying***。

        destroy〔dɪ'strɔɪ〕*v.* 破壞；摧毀

There are stories <u>not just of</u> death and destruction <u>but of</u> strange

                     4   4

scenes — chickens that still survive but with all of their
feathers gone, pieces of straw stuck in trees.

關於龍捲風，不是只有死亡與破壞的故事，還有些奇異的景象——雞隻仍然存活，但所有的羽毛都不見了；一捆捆稻草卡在樹上。

    ** destruction〔dɪ'strʌkʃən〕*n.* 破壞；摧毀

       scene〔sin〕*n.* 場景；景象   survive〔sɚ'vaɪv〕*v.* 存活

       feather〔'fɛðɚ〕*n.* 羽毛   gone〔gɔn〕*adj.* 消失的

       piece〔pis〕*n.* 捆；塊   straw〔strɔ〕*n.* 稻草

       stick〔stɪk〕*v.* 使卡住；使困住【三態變化為：stick-stuck-stuck】

4. (**C**)　not only A but (also) B

　　　　= not just A but (also) B

　　　　不僅 A，而且 B

　　　　又兩個空格中均須有介系詞 of，故選 (C) *not just of* death

　　　　and destruction *but of* strange scenes。

In a 1999 U.S. storm, fierce winds from one tornado lifted a
church into the air and dropped it onto a house.　In the same
storm, a baby was torn from its mother's arms and later found
<u>alive</u> in a nearby tree.
　5
在美國，1999 年的一場暴風雨當中，龍捲風的強勁風勢，將一座教堂
捲至空中，然後又讓它掉到一間民宅上。同一場暴風雨中，有個嬰兒
從母親的臂彎中被扯開，稍後卻發現在附近的樹上，那個嬰兒還活著。

　　** storm〔stɔrm〕*n.* 暴風雨

　　　　fierce〔fɪrs〕*adj.* 兇猛的；強烈的

　　　　the air 空中　　　drop〔drɑp〕*v.* 使落下

　　　　tear〔tɛr〕*v.* 掙開；扯下【三態變化為：tear-tore-torn】

　　　　nearby〔'nɪr͵baɪ〕*adj.* 附近的

5. (**C**)　依句意，被發現還「活著」，「be found + 補語」，故空

　　　　格應填形容詞，又 living（活的），須置於名詞之前，

　　　　如 living things（生物），在此用法不合，而 (B) lively

　　　　〔'laɪvlɪ〕*adj.* 活潑的，(D) lived〔lɪvd , laɪvd〕*adj.*

　　　　（有）…壽命的【常構成複合字，如 long-lived（長命的）】，

　　　　均不合句意，故選 (C) *alive*〔ə'laɪv〕*adj.* 活著的。

TEST 28

Read the following passage and choose the best answer for each blank from the choices below.

Here are some ways to express your creativity. First, be curious about things that you do or use every day. Don't take things ___1___. Ask, "Why are things done the way they are?" Sometimes the best ideas come from combining old ideas or changing them slightly. Second, avoid being immediately ___2___. Write down the idea and think about it for a while. It may be useful later. Don't forget many great inventions came from ideas that seemed impossible at the time. Third, ___3___ just accepting what you know as reality, ask, "What if things were different?" For example, if we ask, "What if everyone could attend university?" we will eventually come to realize that a university diploma wouldn't be as special. Fourth, ___4___ time in your day to relax

and daydream. Sometimes, you may be surprised by
the ideas you have. Last but not least, when you're not
making any ___5___ with your problem, stop working
on it. Do something completely different. Then come
back to the problem. Perhaps you will have a new way
to solve it. Try some of these tips. You may find being
creative isn't hard at all. 【師大附中】

1. (A) for granted   (B) hands-on
   (C) in order   (D) on short notice

2. (A) confident   (B) critical
   (C) interactive   (D) gracious

3. (A) because of   (B) in addition to
   (C) in spite of   (D) instead of

4. (A) make   (B) give
   (C) kill   (D) divide

5. (A) headway   (B) outlook
   (C) glitch   (D) solution

TEST 28 詳解

Here are some ways to express your creativity. First, be
curious about things that you do or use every day. Don't take
things <u>for granted</u>. Ask, "Why are things done the way they are?"
        1
Sometimes the best ideas come from combining old ideas or
changing them slightly.

這裡有一些表達創意的方法。首先,要對每天所做的事或所用的
東西感到好奇。別把事情視爲理所當然。要問:「爲什麼事情是這樣
做呢?」有時候最好的想法,來自於結合舊有的觀念,或者稍微改變
它們。

   ** express〔ɪkˋsprɛs〕*v.* 表達;表現
      creativity〔͵krieˋtɪvətɪ〕*n.* 創意;創造力
      curious〔ˋkjʊrɪəs〕*adj.* 好奇的
      combine〔kəmˋbaɪn〕*v.* 結合   slightly〔ˋslaɪtlɪ〕*adv.* 稍微地

1. (**A**) 依句意,選 (A) *take ~ for granted*「把~視爲理所當然」。
      而 (B) hands-on「實地的;親身實踐的」,(C) take things
      in order「按順序處理事情」,(D) 應改爲 at short notice
      「在短時間內;接到通知後馬上」,皆不合句意。

Second, avoid being immediately <u>critical</u>. Write down the idea
                     2
and think about it for a while. It may be useful later. Don't
forget many great inventions came from ideas that seemed
impossible at the time.

第二，不要立刻批評。把你的想法寫下來，好好思考一下。因為以後可能會有用。別忘了，很多偉大的發明，都來自於當時看來不可能的點子。

** avoid〔ə'vɔɪd〕v. 避免
immediately〔ɪ'midɪɪtlɪ〕*adv.* 立刻；馬上
for a while 一會兒　invention〔ɪn'vɛnʃən〕*n.* 發明

2. (**B**)　(A) confident〔'kɑnfədənt〕*adj.* 有自信的
(B) *critical*〔'krɪtɪkḷ〕*adj.* 好批評的；吹毛求疵的
(C) interactive〔,ɪntɚ'æktɪv〕*adj.* 交互作用的
(D) gracious〔'greʃəs〕*adj.* 親切的；仁慈的

Third, <u>instead of</u> just accepting what you know as reality, ask,
　　　　　　3
"What if things were different?" For example, if we ask, "What if everyone could attend university?" we will eventually come to realize that a university diploma wouldn't be as special.

第三，不要只接受你所知的現況，而是要問：「如果情況不同的話呢？」例如，假使我們問說：「如果每個人都能夠上大學的話，那會怎樣呢？」最後我們就會發現，如此一來大學文憑就沒那麼特別了。

** accept〔ək'sɛpt〕v. 視（為）　*accept* A *as* B 把 A 視為 B
reality〔rɪ'ælətɪ〕*n.* 事實　*What if ~?* 如果～該怎麼辦？
attend〔ə'tɛnd〕v. 上（學）　university〔,junə'vɝsətɪ〕*n.* 大學
eventually〔ɪ'vɛntʃʊəlɪ〕*adv.* 最後；終究
come to V. 開始～　realize〔'rɪə,laɪz〕v. 了解
diploma〔dɪ'plomə〕*n.* 文憑；畢業證書

3. (**D**)　依句意，選 (D) *instead of*「不…而~」。而 (A) because of「因為」，(B) in addition to「除了…之外（還有）」，(C) in spite of「儘管」，皆不合句意。

Fourth, <u>make</u> time in your day to relax and daydream.
    4

Sometimes, you may be surprised by the ideas you have.

第四，在一天當中，停下腳步放鬆，並做做白日夢。有時你可能會
對自己所想到的點子感到吃驚。

     ** relax〔rɪ'læks〕*v.* 放鬆　　daydream〔'deˌdrim〕*v.* 做白日夢
     be surprised by 對…感到驚訝

  4.(**A**)　依句意，選 (A) ***make time***「騰出時間」。而 (C) kill time
        「消磨時間」，則不合句意。

Last but not least, when you're not making any <u>headway</u> with
          5

your problem, stop working on it. Do something completely
different. Then come back to the problem. Perhaps you will
have a new way to solve it. Try some of these tips. You may
find being creative isn't hard at all.

最後一項要點是，當你做某件事情，但卻毫無進展的時候，就先停下
來。去做點完全不同的事。然後再回來處理這個問題。或許你就會有
新的方法來解決它。試試看這些秘訣吧。你可能會發現，要有創意其
實一點也不難。

     ** ***last but not least*** 最後一項要點是；最後但並非最不重要的一點
       completely〔kəm'plitlɪ〕*adv.* 完全地
       come back to 回到　　tip〔tɪp〕*n.* 秘訣
       creative〔krɪ'etɪv〕*adj.* 有創造力的　　***not~at all*** 一點也不~

  5.(**A**)　(A) ***headway***〔'hɛdˌwe〕*n.* 前進　　***make headway*** 進展
      (B) outlook〔'aʊtˌlʊk〕*n.* 看法
      (C) glitch〔glɪtʃ〕*n.* 故障；毛病
      (D) solution〔sə'luʃən〕*n.* 解決之道

TEST 29

Read the following passage and choose the best answer for each
blank from the choices below.

Today there are over 6,000 different languages in the
world. ___1___, many experts predict that the time may soon
come ___2___ most of the languages die out. Two factors
___3___. One is trade, and ___4___ is technology. As we
know, cultures that ___5___ themselves ___5___ international
business and the world community have difficulty ___6___.

1. (A) Therefore   (B) Consequently
   (C) For example   (D) However

2. (A) how   (B) when   (C) why   (D) where

3. (A) are blaming   (B) should blame
   (C) are to blame   (D) have to blame

4. (A) other   (B) another   (C) others   (D) the other

5. (A) separate ; with   (B) isolate ; from
   (C) keep ; up with   (D) prevent ; by

6. (A) to prosper   (B) prospered
   (C) prospering   (D) prosper

As a result, their languages become less common. Technology affects languages in a(n) ___7___ more fascinating way. Modern media ___8___ radio and television give young people a great deal of knowledge about the world. This knowledge usually comes ___9___ the language of a mainstream culture. So it's not surprising that young people are drawn away from their regional languages. 【北一女中】

7. (A) by far (B) the very
   (C) even (D) much the

8. (A) about (B) such
   (C) such as (D) for

9. (A) in (B) by
   (C) with (D) from

TEST 29 詳解

　　Today there are over 6,000 different languages in the world. <u>However</u>, many experts predict that the time may
1

soon come <u>when</u> most of the languages die out. Two factors
2

<u>are to blame</u>. One is trade, and <u>the other</u> is technology.
3　　　　　　　　　　　　　　4

　　現今世上有超過六千種不同的語言。然而,許多專家預測,大多數語言逐漸消失的時刻可能很快就會來到。造成這種結果的因素有兩個。其中之一是貿易,而另一個因素則是科技。

> ** expert〔ˈɛkspɝt〕*n.* 專家
> 　　predict〔prɪˈdɪkt〕*v.* 預測
> 　　***die out*** 逐漸廢除;滅絕
> 　　factor〔ˈfæktɚ〕*n.* 因素　　trade〔tred〕*n.* 貿易
> 　　technology〔tɛkˈnɑlədʒɪ〕*n.* 科技

1. (**D**) 依句意,選 (D) ***However***「然而」。而 (A) 因此,(B) 因此,(C) 例如,均不合句意。

2. (**B**) 表時間,關係副詞用 ***when***,選 (B)。

3. (**C**) ***be to blame*** 該受責備;就是原因

4. (**D**) 兩者中的另一個,須用 ***the other***,選 (D)。而 (A) other「其他的」,(B) another「(三者以上)另一個」,(C) others「其他的人或物」,均不合。

As we know, cultures that <u>isolate</u> themselves <u>from</u> international
　　　　　　　　　　　　　　5　　　　　　　　　　5

business and the world community have difficulty <u>prospering</u>.
　　　　　　　　　　　　　　　　　　　　　　　　　　　6

As a result, their languages become less common.

正如我們所知，將自己隔絕於國際事務及國際社會之外的文化，是
很難蓬勃發展的。因此，他們的語言就會變得比較不普及。

> ** culture (ˈkʌltʃɚ) *n.* 文化
> international (ˌɪntɚˈnæʃənḷ) *adj.* 國際的
> business (ˈbɪznɪs) *n.* 商業；事務
> community (kəˈmjunətɪ) *n.* 社會
> ***world community*** 國際社會　　***as a result*** 因此
> common (ˈkɑmən) *adj.* 普遍的

5. (**B**) ***isolate*** A ***from*** B　使 A 和 B 隔離
　　(A) 須改爲 separate A from B「使 A 和 B 分離」才
　　能選。

6. (**C**) have difficulty + (in) + V-ing「很難～」，選 (C)
　　prospering。　　prosper (ˈprɑspɚ) *v.* 興盛；繁榮

Technology affects languages in an <u>even</u> more fascinating
　　　　　　　　　　　　　　　　　7

way.　Modern media <u>such as</u> radio and television give young
　　　　　　　　　　　8

people a great deal of knowledge about the world.　This

knowledge usually comes <u>in</u> the language of a mainstream
　　　　　　　　　　　　　9

culture.　So it's not surprising that young people are drawn

away from their regional languages.

科技用一種更加吸引人的方法影響語言。像是收音機和電視等現
代媒體，給年輕人很多關於世界的知識。這樣的知識，通常是用
主流文化的語言來呈現。所以年輕人會脫離自己地方性的語言，
就不令人驚訝了。

** affect〔ə'fɛkt〕*v.* 影響
　　fascinating〔'fæsn̩ˌetɪŋ〕*adj.* 吸引人的
　　media〔'midɪə〕*n. pl.* 媒體【單數是 medium】
　　a great deal of 很多的
　　mainstream〔'menˌstrim〕*adj.* 主流的
　　surprising〔sə'praɪzɪŋ〕*adj.* 令人驚訝的
　　draw〔drɔ〕*v.* 引導　　***be drawn away from*** 拋開
　　regional〔'ridʒən̩l〕*adj.* 地方性的

7. (**C**)　修飾比較級，副詞可用：much, even, still 或 far，
　　　　　 故選 (C) ***even***。而 (A) by far the，(B) the very，和
　　　　　 (D) much the 則用於修飾最高級，在此不合。

8. (**C**)　依句意，選 (C) ***such as***「像是」(= *like*)。

9. (**A**)　表「用…語言」，介系詞須用 ***in***，選 (A)。

【劉毅老師的話】

　　「高二英文克漏字測驗」是專為
提昇同學克漏字能力而設計的，你
一定要持之以恆，做完全部四十
回，不可半途而廢。

TEST 30

Read the following passage and choose the best answer for each blank from the choices below.

Many Americans deeply believe that aliens visit the earth regularly. And thousands of them say they ___1___ kidnapped by aliens in the last few years. In fact, there is so much common knowledge about aliens that people can even describe what they look like. Roswell, New Mexico, is ___2___ it all started in 1974. A farmer found shiny material ___3___ over a large area, and then the army took it away. To cover up the truth, they told people that it was something from a weather balloon. People forgot about the ___4___ until the 1980s, when they read several stories about the crashed spaceship and alien bodies.

Now Roswell has become a meeting place for people

who believe in aliens. A lot of people are making

money ___5___ these beliefs by making alien-based

movies and TV talk shows, and selling alien stuff.

【內湖高中】

1. (A) are   (B) have been
   (C) had been   (D) were being

2. (A) where   (B) when
   (C) how   (D) what

3. (A) scattering   (B) to scatter
   (C) scattered   (D) is scattered

4. (A) resident   (B) accident
   (C) incident   (D) precedent

5. (A) from   (B) by
   (C) in   (D) of

TEST 30 詳解

Many Americans deeply believe that aliens visit the earth regularly. And thousands of them say they <u>have been</u>
1

kidnapped by aliens in the last few years. In fact, there is so much common knowledge about aliens that people can even describe what they look like.

許多美國人深信，外星人會定期造訪地球。而且在過去幾年內，他們當中更有數千人，聲稱自己曾被外星人綁架過。事實上，有很多關於外星人的常識，所以人們都能描述外星人的長相。

** deeply〔'diplɪ〕*adv.* 深深地；強烈地
　　alien〔'eljən〕*n.* 外星人
　　regularly〔'rɛgjələlɪ〕*adv.* 定期地
　　kidnap〔'kɪdnæp〕*v.* 綁架　　*in fact* 事實上
　　common knowledge 常識
　　describe〔dɪ'skraɪb〕*v.* 描述；形容

1. (**B**) 依句意爲現在式，故選 (B) *have been kidnapped*「曾
　　經被綁架過」。

Roswell, New Mexico, is <u>where</u> it all started in 1974. A
2

farmer found shiny material <u>scattered</u> over a large area,
3

and then the army took it away.

而這一切都起源於 1974 年，新墨西哥州的羅斯威爾市。有位農夫發現有閃亮的物質，散落在大片的土地上，然後軍隊就將這些物品帶走了。

** Roswell〔'razwɛl〕*n.* 羅斯威爾市【位於新墨西哥州的
羅斯威爾市,在 1974 年發生離奇的飛碟墜毀事件,由於
事實真相眾說紛紜,政府極力掩飾的態度,更讓人相信這
起飛碟墜毀事件的真實性,羅斯威爾也從此成為飛碟迷的
聖地,每年湧進大批想看飛碟的民眾】
New Mexico〔nju'mɛksɪˌko〕*n.* 新墨西哥州
【美國西南部的一州】
shiny〔'ʃaɪnɪ〕*adj.* 閃亮的
material〔mə'tɪrɪəl〕*n.* 物質
army〔'ɑrmɪ〕*n.* 軍隊

2. (**A**) 表地點,關係副詞用 *where*,選 (A)。

3. (**C**) 依句意,閃亮的物質「被散落」在大片的土地上,選
(C) *scattered*。本句是由:A farmer found shiny
material *which was* scattered over a large area, …
省略關代和 be 動詞 which was 而來。
scatter〔'skætɚ〕*v.* 散播;使散佈在各處

To cover up the truth, they told people that it was something
from a weather balloon. People forgot about the incident
                                                    4
until the 1980s, when they read several stories about the
crashed spaceship and alien bodies.
為了掩蓋真相,軍方對民眾說,這些物質是來自於氣象熱氣球。
直到 1980 年代,當人們讀到有關墜毀的太空船,和外星人屍體
的幾則報導時,才想起這起事件。

** ***cover up*** 掩蓋；隱藏　　balloon〔bə'lun〕*n.* 氣球
weather balloon 氣象熱氣球
story〔'storɪ〕*n.* 報導　　crashed〔kræʃt〕*adj.* 墜毀的
spaceship〔'spes,ʃɪp〕*n.* 太空船
body〔'bɑdɪ〕*n.* 屍體

4. (**C**)　(A) resident〔'rɛzədənt〕*n.* 居民
　　　　　　(B) accident〔'æksədənt〕*n.* 意外；事故
　　　　　　(C) ***incident***〔'ɪnsədənt〕*n.* 事件
　　　　　　(D) precedent〔'prɛsədənt〕*n.* 先例

Now Roswell has become a meeting place for people who
believe in aliens. A lot of people are making money from
　　　　　　　　　　　　　　　　　　　　　　　　　5
these beliefs by making alien-based movies and TV talk
shows, and selling alien stuff.

現在，羅斯威爾市已成為相信有外星人的民眾的聚會地點。很多
人因為大家相信有外星人而賺錢，他們拍攝以外星人為主的電影
跟電視脫口秀節目，並且販賣和外星人有關的東西。

** ***meeting place*** 聚會地點　　***believe in*** 相信有
make money 賺錢　　belief〔bɪ'lif〕*n.* 信念；確信
alien-based〔'eljən'best〕*adj.* 以外星人為基礎的
talk show 脫口秀　　stuff〔stʌf〕*n.* 東西；物品

5. (**A**)　表「從…；由…」來賺錢，選 (A) make money ***from***。
　　　　　　而如要選 (B) by，則須將句子改成：…are making
　　　　　　money ***by*** making alien-based movies…，才能選。

TEST 31

*Read the following passage and choose the best answer for each
blank from the choices below.*

If you are a bargain ___1___, you should never

miss a flea market. In America, flea markets often

operate between 6:00 a.m. and 4:00 p.m. on weekends,

___2___ open spaces such as parking lots, football

fields, or local parks. For most of the vendors

there, the flea market is just a way ___3___ some

extra cash. That's why you might find housewives

___4___ to dispose of baby supplies in a flea market.

1. (A) predator   (B) hunter
   (C) gambler   (D) collector

2. (A) used   (B) using
   (C) use   (D) they use

3. (A) in getting   (B) to get
   (C) for getting   (D) that get

4. (A) try   (B) tried
   (C) to try   (D) trying

When you arrive, you'll find aisles __5__ odds and ends: comic books, shoes, garden tools, and just about anything else you can think of. Food here is cheaper and __6__ than what you'll get at the supermarket. If you come later in the day, you may have a better chance of bargaining with the vendors. After a day of shopping, you will still have money __7__ over. Yes, a flea market is a place __8__ you can wander for acres, see interesting people, and choose __9__ a hodgepodge of goods. Why not come and enjoy the fun of shopping? 【陽明高中】

5. (A) lined with   (B) filled up
   (C) involved in   (D) standing out

6. (A) well-tasted   (B) good-taste
   (C) nice-tasting   (D) better-tasting

7. (A) left   (B) leave   (C) leaving   (D) to leave

8. (A) where   (B) when   (C) which   (D) what

9. (A) with   (B) for   (C) between   (D) from

TEST 31 詳解

If you are a bargain <u>hunter</u>, you should never miss a flea
　　　　　　　　　　 1
market. In America, flea markets often operate between 6:00
a.m. and 4:00 p.m. on weekends, <u>using</u> open spaces such as
　　　　　　　　　　　　　　　　 2
parking lots, football fields, or local parks.

如果你是個喜歡找廉價商品的人，你絕不該錯過跳蚤市場。在美
國，跳蚤市場通常是週末的早上六點營業到下午四點，利用開闊的
空間，像是停車場、足球場，或是當地的公園。

** bargain〔'bɑrgɪn〕*adj.* 廉價的　*v.* 討價還價
　　miss〔mɪs〕*v.* 錯過　　flea〔fli〕*n.* 跳蚤
　　flea market 跳蚤市場　　operate〔'ɑpə,ret〕*v.* 運作；經營
　　open〔'opən〕*adj.* 開闊的　　*parking lot* 停車場
　　football field 足球場　　local〔'lokl̩〕*adj.* 當地的

1. (**B**)　依句意，選 (B) *bargain hunter*「搜尋廉價貨的人」。
　　　　hunter〔'hʌntɚ〕*n.* 獵人；搜尋…的人
　　　　而 (A) predator〔'prɛdətɚ〕*n.* 捕食者，(C) gambler
　　　　〔'gæmblɚ〕*n.* 賭徒，(D) collector〔kə'lɛktɚ〕*n.* 收集者；
　　　　收藏者，則不合句意。

2. (**B**)　兩動詞中無連接詞，第二個動詞須改成現在分詞，故選 (B)
　　　　using。

For most of the vendors there, the flea market is just a way
<u>to get</u> some extra cash. That's why you might find housewives
 3
<u>trying</u> to dispose of baby supplies in a flea market.
 4

對於那裡的大部分攤販而言，跳蚤市場只是個賺取額外現金的方法。
這就是為什麼你可以看到家庭主婦，想在跳蚤市場中，處理掉一些嬰
兒用品。

> ** vendor〔'vɛndɚ〕*n.* 小販　　extra〔'ɛkstrə〕*adj.* 額外的
> cash〔kæʃ〕*n.* 現金　　dispose〔dɪ'spoz〕*v.* 處置 < *of* >
> supplies〔sə'plaɪz〕*n. pl.* 生活用品

3. (**B**)　依句意，選 (B) *a way to V.*「一個~的方法」。

4. (**D**)　*find sb.* + *V-ing* 發現某人正在~

When you arrive, you'll find aisles <u>lined with</u> odds and ends:
5
comic books, shoes, garden tools, and just about anything else
you can think of.　Food here is cheaper and <u>better-tasting</u> than
6
what you'll get at the supermarket.
當你抵達時，你會發現沿著走道，排滿了許多雜物：漫畫書、鞋子、
園藝用的工具，幾乎任何你想得到的東西都有。這裡的食物比較便
宜，而且比你在超級市場買的還要好吃。

> ** arrive〔ə'raɪv〕*v.* 到達　　aisle〔aɪl〕*n.* 通道
> ***odds and ends*** 零星雜物　　***comic book*** 漫畫書
> garden〔'gɑrdn̩〕*adj.* 園藝用的　　tool〔tul〕*n.* 工具
> ***just about*** 差不多；幾乎 (= *almost*)　　***think of*** 想到

5. (**A**)　依句意，沿著走道，「排滿了」許多雜物，選 (A) ***lined with***。
line〔laɪn〕*v.* 將…排成一列；沿…排列
而 (B) fill up「填滿」，(C) be involved in「牽涉在…當中；
和…有關」，(D) stand out「突出；傑出」，則不合句意。

6. (**D**)　「好吃的」是 good-tasting，所以「較好吃的」就是
better-tasting，選 (D)。

If you come later in the day, you may have a better chance of bargaining with the vendors. After a day of shopping, you will still have money <u>left</u> over.
　　　　　　　　　　　　　　7

如果你當天來得比較晚，你比較有機會跟攤販討價還價。買了一整天之後，你的錢還會有剩。

　　** later〔'letɚ〕*adv.* 較晚

7. (**A**) 依句意，仍然有錢剩下，應用被動語態，選 (A) *left*。
　　　　本句是由：…you will still have money *which is left*
　　　　over. 省略關代和 be 動詞 which was，簡化而來。
　　　　leave over 剩下；留下【常用被動語態】

Yes, a flea market is a place <u>where</u> you can wander for acres,
　　　　　　　　　　　　　　　　　8
see interesting people, and choose <u>from</u> a hodgepodge of goods.
　　　　　　　　　　　　　　　9
Why not come and enjoy the fun of shopping?

沒錯，跳蚤市場是個你可以逛上好幾英畝，看看有趣的人，並且從一大堆混雜在一起的商品中挑選物品的地方。何不一起來享受購物的樂趣呢？

　　** wander〔'wɑndɚ〕*v.* 徘徊；閒蕩；到處走
　　　acre〔'ekɚ〕*n.* 英畝　　hodgepodge〔'hɑdʒ,pɑdʒ〕*n.* 混雜
　　　goods〔gʊdz〕*n. pl.* 商品　　***why not V.*** 何不…

8. (**A**) 表地點，關係副詞用 ***where***，選 (A)。

9. (**D**) 依句意，「從…中」挑選，選 (D) ***from***。而 (C) between 指「在（兩者）之間」，在此不合句意。

TEST 32

Read the following passage and choose the best answer for each blank from the choices below.

When Levi Strauss arrived in the United States from Bavaria, he was only seventeen, poor, and knew very ___1___ English. Like most other ___2___, he was looking for a better life. So when gold was discovered in the West in 1849, he ___3___ thousands of others and rushed to California. ___4___ he planned to open a shop in San Francisco, he took many goods with him, ___5___ a lot of canvas. He hoped to sell ___6___ for tents and wagon covers. Business, however, was not as ___7___ as he had expected. ___8___, as he sat in a café in a small town, he had an idea. He saw a man with a hole in the leg of his pants and suddenly realized what Californians ___9___ for the rough work they were doing — good, strong ___10___. 【恆毅高中】

1. (A) easy   (B) some
   (C) small   (D) little

2. (A) demonstrators   (B) marchers
   (C) immigrants   (D) tailors

3. (A) took   (B) entered
   (C) paid   (D) joined

4. (A) Although   (B) Because
   (C) If   (D) Unless

5. (A) including   (B) included
   (C) being included   (D) was including

6. (A) it   (B) one
   (C) them   (D) others

7. (A) far   (B) good
   (C) soon   (D) well

8. (A) One day   (B) Another day
   (C) Some day   (D) The other day

9. (A) needed   (B) need
   (C) needing   (D) have needed

10. (A) shirts   (B) jackets
    (C) coats   (D) pants

TEST 32 詳解

When Levi Strauss arrived in the United States from Bavaria, he was only seventeen, poor, and knew very <u>little</u> English.
₁

當李維・史特勞斯從巴伐利亞到美國時，他只有十七歲，當時他很窮，而且只懂一點點英文。

** Levi Strauss〔'livaɪ'straus〕*n.* 李維・史特勞斯
【牛仔褲的發明者】　　***arrive in*** 到達
Bavaria〔bə'vɛrɪə〕*n.* 巴伐利亞【德國南部地名】

1. (**D**) 依句意，選 (D) ***little*** 「很少」。

Like most other <u>immigrants</u>, he was looking for a better life.
₂
So when gold was discovered in the West in 1849, he <u>joined</u>
₃
thousands of others and rushed to California.

他像許多其他的移民一樣，想尋找更好的生活。所以當 1849 年，美國西部發現黃金的時候，他就加入數以千計的民眾，趕往加州。

** discover〔dɪ'skʌvɚ〕*v.* 發現
the West （美國）西部各州【從密西西比河到太平洋沿岸各州】
rush〔rʌʃ〕*v.* 匆忙趕往　　California〔ˌkælə'fɔrnjə〕*n.* 加州

2. (**C**) (A) demonstrator〔'dɛmənˌstretɚ〕*n.* 示威者
(B) marcher〔'mɑrtʃɚ〕*n.* 遊行者
(C) ***immigrant***〔'ɪməgrənt〕*n.* （來自外國的）移民
(D) tailor〔'telɚ〕*n.* 裁縫師

3. (**D**)　依句意，選 (D) *joined*「加入」。而 (A) take「帶著」，
　　　　　(B) enter「進入」，(C) pay「付（錢）」，則不合句意。

<u>Because</u> he planned to open a shop in San Francisco, he took
　　4

many goods with him, <u>including</u> a lot of canvas.　He hoped to
　　　　　　　　　　　5

sell <u>it</u> for tents and wagon covers.　Business, however, was
　　　6

not as <u>good</u> as he had expected.
　　　　7

因為他計畫要在舊金山開一間店，所以隨身帶了許多商品，包括很多
帆布。他希望能販賣帆布，作為帳棚或四輪馬車的車頂遮蓋布。但是，
生意並沒有他預期的那麼好。

　　** San Francisco〔͵sænfrən'sɪsko〕*n.* 舊金山
　　　　goods〔gʊdz〕*n. pl.* 商品；貨物　　canvas〔'kænvəs〕*n.* 帆布
　　　　tent〔tɛnt〕*n.* 帳棚　　wagon〔'wægən〕*n.* 四輪馬車
　　　　cover〔'kʌvɚ〕*n.* 遮蓋物　　expect〔ɪk'spɛkt〕*v.* 預期

4. (**B**)　依句意，選 (B) *Because*「因為」。而 (A) 雖然，(C) 如果，
　　　　　(D) 除非，均不合句意。

5. (**A**)　依句意，「包括」許多帆布，選 (A) *including*。而 (B) 須改
　　　　　為 and included 才能選。

6. (**A**)　依句意，希望能賣 canvas（帆布），由於 canvas 為不可數
　　　　　名詞，故代名詞用 *it*，選 (A)。

7. (**B**)　依句意，生意不如他預期的「好」，須填形容詞，選 (B)
　　　　　good。

<u>One day</u>, as he sat in a cafe in a small town, he had an idea.
   8

He saw a man with a hole in the leg of his pants and suddenly

realized what Californians <u>needed</u> for the rough work they
       9

were doing — good, strong <u>pants</u>.
       10

有一天，當他坐在小鎮上的露天咖啡座時，他想到一個點子。他看到
一個男人，穿著一條褲管上有破洞的褲子，然後他突然領悟，加州人
做粗重工作時所需要的東西——好穿又堅固的長褲。

  ** café〔kə'fe〕*n.* 露天咖啡座   hole〔hol〕*n.* 洞

     leg〔lɛg〕*n.* 褲管   pants〔pænts〕*n. pl.* 褲子

     realize〔'riə‚laɪz〕*v.* 了解；知道

     Californian〔‚kælə'fɔrnjən〕*n.* 加州人

     rough〔rʌf〕*adj.* 粗重的；費勞力的

     strong〔strɔŋ〕*adj.* 牢固的

8.(**A**) 依句意，選 (A)***One day***「（過去、將來）有一天」。而
        (B) another day「另一天」，(D) the other day「前幾
        天」，則不合句意；(C) some day「（將來）有一天」，
        用於未來式，在此不合。

9.(**A**) 空格應填動詞，依句意為過去式，故選 (A)***needed***。

10.(**D**) 依句意，選 (D)***pants***「褲子」。而 (A) 襯衫，(B) 夾克，
        (C) 外套，皆不合句意。

TEST 33

Read the following passage and choose the best answer for each blank from the choices below.

Dear Terry,

How is everything going? School has started again and you must ___1___ a wonderful summer vacation.

You told me you were curious about ___2___ high school life was like in Taiwan. To make a long story short, schoolwork is the top ___3___ for us. The heavy pressure of schoolwork ___4___ us hardly any time for recreation. ___5___ their age or occupation, most of our parents have one thing in common — the hope that we can get into a good university.

1. (A) be spent   (B) spend   (C) have spent   (D) spending

2. (A) whether   (B) which   (C) how   (D) what

3. (A) priority   (B) distraction
   (C) treatment   (D) performance

4. (A) makes   (B) leaves   (C) brings   (D) lets

5. (A) Apart from   (B) According to
   (C) Based on   (D) Regardless of

Take my parents for example. They discourage me ___6___ "wasting" time on any activities that have nothing to do with my studies. As a result, whenever I am ___7___ playing computer games or reading comic books, they start preaching to me about my idleness. Without any exception, they conclude by reminding me that if I fail to score high on the entrance exam, I will end up ___8___ a nobody in the future. In a word, they hope I will try my best to live up to their expectations.

Well, I have to burn the midnight oil studying for my mid-term exams. They're only a week ___9___. If I am not on the list of the top 50 students, I'll be ___10___ on weekends.

Give my best regards to your family.

Your e-pal,

Kevin

【延平高中】

6. (A) by   (B) to   (C) with   (D) from

7. (A) forbidden   (B) allowed   (C) scolded   (D) caught

8. (A) with   (B) as   (C) in   (D) to

9. (A) ago   (B) away   (C) later   (D) after

10. (A) grounded   (B) persuaded   (C) furnished   (D) explored

TEST 33 詳解

Dear Terry,

How is everything going? School has started again and you must <u>have spent</u> a wonderful summer vacation.
1

親愛的泰瑞：

最近過得好嗎？學校又開學了，你一定過了一個很棒的暑假。

** *school starts* 開學　　wonderful (ˈwʌndəfəl) *adj.* 很棒的

1. (**C**) 依句意，對過去肯定的推測，須用 *must have + p.p.* 表「當時一定～」，故選 (C)。

You told me you were curious about <u>what</u> high school life
2
was like in Taiwan. To make a long story short, schoolwork is the top <u>priority</u> for us. The heavy pressure of schoolwork <u>leaves</u>
3　　　　　　　　　　　　　　　　　　　4
us hardly any time for recreation.

你說你很好奇，台灣的高中生活是怎樣。簡單來說，學校課業是我們的第一要務。沉重的課業壓力，讓我們幾乎沒有休閒娛樂的時間。

** curious (ˈkjʊrɪəs) *adj.* 好奇的；想知道的
　　to make a long story short 長話短說；簡言之
　　schoolwork (ˈskul͵wɝk) *n.* 功課；學業（成績）
　　pressure (ˈprɛʃɚ) *n.* 壓力　　hardly (ˈhɑrdlɪ) *adv.* 幾乎不
　　recreation (͵rɛkrɪˈeʃən) *n.* 娛樂；消遣

2. (**D**) *what ~ is like* ～如何

3. (**A**) 依句意，選 (A) *top priority*「最優先的事」。
　　priority (praɪˈɔrətɪ) *n.* 優先的事物

而 (B) distraction〔dɪˈstrækʃən〕*n.* 使人分心的事物，
(C) treatment〔ˈtritmənt〕*n.* 治療，(D) performance
〔pɚˈfɔrməns〕*n.* 表演；表現，則不合句意。

4. (**B**) 依句意，選 (B) *leaves*「留給（某人）～」。

<u>Regardless of</u> their age or occupation, most of our parents have
     5
one thing in common — the hope that we can get into a good
university.　Take my parents for example.　They discourage me
<u>from</u> "wasting" time on any activities that have nothing to do
  6
with my studies.
大部分台灣高中生的父母不論年齡或職業，都有個共通點——希望我們
能夠進入好大學。以我的父母爲例。他們阻止我把時間「浪費」在任
何與課業無關的活動上。

  ** occupation〔ˌɑkjəˈpeʃən〕*n.* 職業
    have one thing in common 有一個共同點
    take sb. for example 以某人爲例
    discourage〔dɪsˈkɝɪdʒ〕*v.* 阻止；反對 < *from* >
    have nothing to do with 和…無關
    studies〔ˈstʌdɪz〕*n. pl.* 學業；課業

5. (**D**) 「不論」是什麼年紀或職業，選 (D) *Regardless of*「不管；
不論；不分」。而 (A) apart from「除了…之外」，(B)
according to「根據」，(C) based on「根據」，則不合句意。

6. (**D**) *discourage sb. from V-ing* 阻止某人做～

As a result, whenever I am <u>caught</u> playing computer games or
       7
reading comic books, they start preaching to me about my

idleness. Without any exception, they conclude by reminding
me that if I fail to score high on the entrance exam, I will end
up <u>as</u> a nobody in the future. In a word, they hope I will try
　　8
my best to live up to their expectations.

因此，每當我被抓到正在玩電腦遊戲，或是看漫畫，他們就開始教訓
我，說我遊手好閒。他們每次都會在最後提醒我說，假如我在入學考試
中失敗，那我以後就只是個無名小卒。總之，他們希望我能全力以赴，
以符合他們的期望。

　　** ***as a result*** 因此　　***computer game*** 電腦遊戲
　　comic books 漫畫書　　preach〔prit∫〕*v.* 訓誡；說教
　　idleness〔'aɪdḷnɪs〕*n.* 遊手好閒
　　exception〔ɪk'sɛp∫ən〕*n.* 例外　　***without exception*** 無例外地
　　conclude〔kən'klud〕*v.* 總結；結束
　　remind〔rɪ'maɪnd〕*v.* 提醒　　***fail to V.*** 未能～
　　score〔skor〕*v.* 得分　　***score high*** 得高分
　　entrance〔'ɛntrəns〕*n.* 進入；入學
　　entrance exam 入學考試　　***in a word*** 總之
　　try one's ***best*** 盡力　　***live up to*** 符合（期望）
　　expectations〔ˌɛkspɛk'te∫ənz〕*n. pl.* 期望

7. (**D**)　依句意，選 (D) ***be caught + V-ing***「被抓到在～；被當場
　　　　撞見正在～」。而 (A) forbid〔fɚ'bɪd〕*v.* 禁止，(B) allow
　　　　「允許」，(C) scold〔skold〕*v.* 責罵，用法與句意均不合。

8. (**B**)　a nobody「無名小卒」是「身份」，故介系詞用 ***as***，選 (B)。
　　　　end up as 最後成為～
　　　　而 (A) end up with「以～作為結束」，如 end up with a
　　　　speech（以演說結束），(C) end up in「最後變成」，如
　　　　end up in prison（最後被關進監獄），則用法不合。

Well, I have to burn the midnight oil studying for my
mid-term exams. They're only a week <u>away</u>. If I am not on
9

the list of the top 50 students, I'll be <u>grounded</u> on weekends.
10

Give my best regards to your family.

Your e-pal,
Kevin

　　嗯，我必須熬夜唸書準備期中考了，只剩一週就要考試了。如果
我沒有考進前五十名，我週末會被禁足。

　　替我問候你的家人。

你的網友，
凱文

** ***burn the midnight oil*** 熬夜
　　mid-term〔'mɪd'tɜm〕*adj.* 學期中的　　list〔lɪst〕*n.* 名單
　　top〔tɑp〕*adj.* 最上面的；最高的
　　regards〔rɪ'gɑrdz〕*n. pl.* （書信等的）問候【例如：Give him my
　　　　(best) regards.（請代我向他問候。）】
　　e-pal〔'i͵pæl〕*n.* 網友（= *electronic pal*）

9.(**B**)　依句意，還剩一個禮拜，選 (B) ***away***「離…有一定時間」。
　　　　a week away 還有一個禮拜
　　　　而 (A)「時間 + ago」，表「（多久）之前」，(C)「時間 +
　　　　later」，表「～之後」，(D) after「在…之後」，為介系詞，
　　　　在此用法均不合。

10.(**A**)　(A) ***ground***〔graʊnd〕*v.* 禁足
　　　　(B) persuade〔pɚ'swed〕*v.* 說服
　　　　(C) furnish〔'fɜnɪʃ〕*v.* 給…裝置傢俱
　　　　(D) explore〔ɪk'splor〕*v.* 探險；探索

TEST 34

*Read the following passage and choose the best answer for each
blank from the choices below.*

When asked about the most popular tourist spots
in Paris, in addition to the Eiffel Tower and the Louvre
Museum, most people mention the Pompidou Center.
Constructed in the 1970s, the Pompidou Center is
known for being an ___1___ masterpiece which
houses many delicate modern works of art. ___2___,
in the beginning it failed to appeal to most Paris residents
due to its peculiar and revolutionary appearance,
which made it look more like a construction site
than a museum. All the pipes, escalators and
supporting structures are placed outside the walls.

1. (A) archaeological   (B) anthropological
   (C) architectural   (D) astrological

2. (A) Fortunately   (B) Likewise
   (C) Furthermore   (D) Nevertheless

The dislike of its ___3___ design came to an end in 1977 when the Pompidou Center was officially introduced to Paris, and it began to enjoy its ___4___ popularity. In addition to its impressive look and large collection of artistic pieces, the Pompidou Center also ___5___ a square named Place Beaubourg, where small carnivals can be arranged, fantastic shows can be put on and the relaxed crowd can be entertained. The Pompidou Center is sure to get your vote as one of the most memorable art centers in the world. 【大同高中】

3. (A) interior   (B) exterior
   (C) chronological   (D) conscious

4. (A) long-last   (B) long-lasted
   (C) long-lasting   (D) long-lasts

5. (A) features   (B) symbolizes
   (C) reflects   (D) produces

TEST 34 詳解

When asked about the most popular tourist spots in Paris, in addition to the Eiffel Tower and the Louvre Museum, most people mention the Pompidou Center. Constructed in the 1970s, the Pompidou Center is known for being an <u>architectural</u>

1

masterpiece which houses many delicate modern works of art.

當問到巴黎最受歡迎的觀光景點是哪裡的時候，除了艾菲爾鐵塔跟羅浮宮博物館之外，大多數的人會提到龐畢度中心。龐畢度中心是在 1970 年代建造的，它是有名的建築上的傑作，裡面收藏許多精緻的現代藝術品。

** *tourist spot* 觀光景點

in addition to 除了…之外（還有）

Eiffel Tower ('aɪfḷ'tauɚ) *n.* 艾菲爾鐵塔

Louvre Museum ('luvɚˏmju'ziəm) *n.* 羅浮宮【原是法國皇宮，1793 年改建為博物館，館藏多達 40 萬件】

mention ('mɛnʃən) *v.* 提到

Pompidou Center ('pɑmpɪdu'sɛntɚ) *n.* 龐畢度中心【位於巴黎 Beaubourg 區的藝術中心，為紀念二次大戰勝利而建造，1977 年開幕】

construct (kən'strʌkt) *v.* 建造

be known for 以…而聞名

masterpiece ('mæstɚˏpis) *n.* 傑作

house (hauz) *v.* 收藏　　delicate ('dɛləkət) *adj.* 精緻的

work of art 藝術品

1. (**C**) (A) archaeological〔͵ɑrkɪə'lɑdʒɪkḷ〕*adj.* 考古學的

   (B) anthropological〔͵ænθrəpə'lɑdʒɪkḷ〕*adj.* 人類學的

   (C) *architectural*〔͵ɑrkə'tɛktʃərəl〕*adj.* 建築上的

   (D) astrological〔͵æstrə'lɑdʒɪkḷ〕*adj.* 占星術的

<u>Nevertheless</u>, in the beginning it failed to appeal to most Paris
    2
residents due to its peculiar and revolutionary appearance,
which made it look more like a construction site than a museum.
All the pipes, escalators and supporting structures are placed
outside the walls. The dislike of its <u>exterior</u> design came to an
                                            3
end in 1977 when the Pompidou Center was officially introduced
to Paris, and it began to enjoy its <u>long-lasting</u> popularity.
                                         4

儘管如此,一開始,它並不吸引大多數的巴黎居民,因為它奇特又顛
覆傳統的外觀,使它看起來比較像建築工地,而不像博物館。所有的
管線、手扶梯,和附屬結構都被放在牆外。對龐畢度中心外觀的厭惡,
就在 1977 年它正式在巴黎亮相時結束,龐畢度中心開始受到長期的
歡迎。

   ** *fail to V.* 未能…

    appeal to 吸引　　resident〔'rɛzədənt〕*n.* 居民

    due to 由於　　peculiar〔pɪ'kjuljɚ〕*adj.* 奇特的

    revolutionary〔͵rɛvə'luʃən͵ɛrɪ〕*adj.* 革命性的;顛覆性的

    appearance〔ə'pɪrəns〕*n.* 外觀

    construction〔kən'strʌkʃən〕*n.* 建築;施工

    a construction site 建築工地　　pipe〔paɪp〕*n.* 管線

    escalator〔'ɛskə͵letɚ〕*n.* 手扶梯

supporting〔 sə'portɪŋ 〕*adj.* 輔助的；支撐的

structure〔'strʌktʃɚ 〕*n.* 構造；建築物

place〔 ples 〕*v.* 放置

dislike〔 dɪs'laɪk 〕*n.* 厭惡　　***come to an end*** 結束

officially〔 ə'fɪʃəlɪ 〕*adv.* 正式地

be introduced to 被介紹給；被推薦給；引進

popularity〔ˌpɑpjə'lærətɪ 〕*n.* 受歡迎

2. (**D**) (A) fortunately〔'fɔrtʃənɪtlɪ 〕*adv.* 幸運地

(B) likewise〔'laɪkˌwaɪz 〕*adv.* 同樣地

(C) furthermore〔'fɜðɚˌmor 〕*adv.* 此外

(D) ***nevertheless***〔ˌnɛvɚðə'lɛs 〕*adv.* 然而；儘管如此

3. (**B**) (A) interior〔 ɪn'tɪrɪɚ 〕*adj.* 內部的

(B) ***exterior***〔 ɪk'stɪrɪɚ 〕*adj.* 外部的

(C) chronological〔ˌkrɑnə'lɑdʒɪkl̩ 〕*adj.* 按年代順序的

(D) conscious〔'kɑnʃəs 〕*adj.* 知道的；察覺到的

4. (**C**)　依句意，選 (C) ***long-lasting***「持久的」。

In addition to its impressive look and large collection of artistic pieces, the Pompidou Center also <u>features</u> a square named
　　　　　　　　　　　　　　　　　　　　　　　5
Place Beaubourg, where small carnivals can be arranged, fantastic shows can be put on and the relaxed crowd can be entertained. The Pompidou Center is sure to get your vote as one of the most memorable art centers in the world.

除了令人印象深刻的外觀，以及大量的美術收藏品之外，龐畢度中心更大的特色是波堡廣場，在廣場內，可以籌畫小型的嘉年華會、舉辦很棒的展覽，並且娛樂來到這裡放鬆的群眾。龐畢度中心確實值得你選它作為世界上最令人難忘的藝術中心之一。

> ** impressive〔ɪm'prɛsɪv〕*adj.* 令人印象深刻的
>
> look〔lʊk〕*n.* 外表；樣子
>
> large〔lɑrdʒ〕*adj.*（數量）大的；規模大的
>
> collection〔kə'lɛkʃən〕*n.* 收藏品
>
> artistic〔ɑr'tɪstɪk〕*adj.* 藝術的　　piece〔pis〕*n.* 作品
>
> square〔skwɛr〕*n.* 廣場　　*named*～ 名叫～
>
> Place Beaubourg〔'ples'boˌbur〕*n.* 波堡廣場
>
> carnival〔'kɑrnəvḷ〕*n.* 嘉年華會
>
> arrange〔ə'rendʒ〕*v.* 安排；籌備
>
> fantastic〔fæn'tæstɪk〕*adj.* 很棒的　　*put on* 舉辦
>
> relaxed〔rɪ'lækst〕*adj.* 放鬆的　　crowd〔kraʊd〕*n.* 群眾
>
> entertain〔ˌɛntɚ'ten〕*v.* 娛樂
>
> *be sure to* + *V.* 必定～　　vote〔vot〕*n.* 選票
>
> memorable〔'mɛmərəbḷ〕*adj.* 令人難忘的

5. (**A**)　(A) *feature*〔'fitʃɚ〕*v.* 以～為特色

　　　　　(B) symbolize〔'sɪmbḷˌaɪz〕*v.* 象徵

　　　　　(C) reflect〔rɪ'flɛkt〕*v.* 反射

　　　　　(D) produce〔prə'djus〕*v.* 生產；製造

TEST 35

*Read the following passage and choose the best answer for each
blank from the choices below.*

People all over the world give gifts, but they don't do
it __1__ the same way. In some countries, the wrong gift
can make your good intentions __2__. An appropriate
gift __3__ in the wrong way can also cause you trouble.
Therefore, it's important to understand the etiquette of
gift giving in other cultures. In Japan, for example,
gifts __4__ appreciation and respect. Gifts must be
given __5__ many occasions and are often expensive.

1. (A) at   (B) in   (C) on   (D) to

2. (A) backbite   (B) backfire
   (C) backslide   (D) backtrack

3. (A) gives   (B) giving
   (C) given   (D) which gave

4. (A) are symbolic of   (B) symbolizing
   (C) are symbol to   (D) symbolized

5. (A) at   (B) in   (C) on   (D) with

___6___, Japanese take special care with wrapping to express respect for the recipient. At the other extreme, gift giving in Russia is ___7___. Russians love exchanging gifts and will do so at any time. Gifts are ___8___ tokens of friendship. If you're traveling abroad, don't let gift-giving customs ___9___ you ___9___. Find out about the etiquette in the country you'll be visiting. The right gift, given in the right way, can go a long way toward ___10___ new friendships.

【延平高中】

6. (A) In addition to   (B) However
    (C) Moreover   (D) Despite

7. (A) instantaneous   (B) miscellaneous
    (C) spontaneous   (D) simultaneous

8. (A) thought as   (B) viewed as
    (C) referred to   (D) looked as

9. (A) trip ; up   (B) trick ; on
    (C) burn ; down   (D) lay ; off

10. (A) build   (B) cement
     (C) interacting   (D) strengthening

TEST 35 詳解

People all over the world give gifts, but they don't do it <u>in</u>

                                                                            1
the same way. In some countries, the wrong gift can make your
good intentions <u>backfire</u>.

                      2

全世界的人都會送禮，但方式各不相同。在某些國家，不適當的禮
物可能會使你的好意有相反的效果。

** intention〔ɪn'tɛnʃən〕 *n.* 企圖；用意

1. (**B**)　表「用…方式」，介系詞須用 ***in***，選 (B)。

2. (**B**)　好意可能會「產生適得其反的結果」，選 (B) ***backfire***
　　　　　〔'bæk,faɪr〕 *v.*。而 (A) backbite〔'bæk,baɪt〕 *v.* 背後說壞話，
　　　　　(C) backslide〔'bæk,slaɪd〕 *v.* 退步；墮落，(D) backtrack
　　　　　〔'bæk,træk〕 *v.* 由原路退回，則不合句意。

An appropriate gift <u>given</u> in the wrong way can also cause you

                                   3
trouble. Therefore, it's important to understand the etiquette
of gift giving in other cultures.

一份適當的禮物，如果用錯誤的方法送，也可能會給你帶來麻煩。因
此，了解其他文化的送禮的禮儀是很重要的。

** appropriate〔ə'proprɪɪt〕 *adj.* 適當的
　　cause〔kɔz〕 *v.* 導致；給…帶來
　　etiquette〔'ɛtɪ,kɛt〕 *n.* 禮儀

3.(**C**) 原句爲：An appropriate gift *which is given* in the wrong way…，關代和 be 動詞可同時省略，故選 (C) *given*。

In Japan, for example, gifts <u>are symbolic of</u> appreciation and
4
respect. Gifts must be given <u>on</u> many occasions and are often
5
expensive. <u>Moreover</u>, Japanese take special care with wrapping
6
to express respect for the recipient.

例如，在日本，禮物象徵感激與敬意。在很多場合都必須送禮，而且禮物常常很貴重。此外，日本人特別注重包裝，用以表達對收禮者的敬意。

** appreciation 〔 ə͵priʃɪ'eʃən 〕 *n.* 感激
respect 〔 rɪ'spɛkt 〕 *n.* 敬意　　occasion 〔 ə'keʒən 〕 *n.* 場合
take care with + *V-ing*　在…方面很注意
wrap 〔 ræp 〕 *v.* 包裝　　express 〔 ɪk'sprɛs 〕 *v.* 表達
recipient 〔 rɪ'sɪpɪənt 〕 *n.* 接受者

4.(**A**) 禮物「象徵」感激與敬意，選 (A) *are symbolic of*。而 (B) (D) 須改爲 symbolize 〔'sɪmbḷ͵aɪz 〕 *v.* 象徵，(C) 須改爲 are the symbol of「是…的象徵」，才能選。

5.(**C**) 表「在…場合」，用 *on…occasion*，選 (C)。

6.(**C**) 依句意，選 (C) *Moreover*「此外」。而 (A) in addition to「除了…之外（還有）」，(B) however「然而」，(D) despite「儘管」，爲介系詞，用法與句意均不合。

At the other extreme, gift giving in Russia is <u>spontaneous</u>.
7

Russians love exchanging gifts and will do so at any time.

Gifts are <u>viewed as</u> tokens of friendship.
8

另一個極端的例子是，在俄國，送禮物是自發性的。俄國人喜歡交換
禮物，而且會在任何時候做。禮物被視爲友誼的象徵。

**　** extreme〔ɪkˈstrim〕*n.* 極端例子

Russia〔ˈrʌʃə〕*n.* 俄國

Russian〔ˈrʌʃən〕*n.* 俄國人　　　token〔ˈtokən〕*n.* 象徵

7. (**C**)　(A) instantaneous〔͵ɪnstənˈtenɪəs〕*adj.* 瞬間的；立即的

(B) miscellaneous〔͵mɪsḷˈenɪəs〕*adj.* 各種各樣的

(C) ***spontaneous***〔spɑnˈtenɪəs〕*adj.* 自發性的；
自然發生的

(D) simultaneous〔͵saɪmḷˈtenɪəs〕*adj.* 同時的；
同時發生的

8. (**B**)　表「被視爲；被認爲是」的說法有：

$$\begin{cases} \text{be thought of as} \\ = \text{be looked upon as} \\ = \text{be regarded as} \end{cases}$$

$$\begin{cases} = \text{be viewed as} \\ = \text{be seen as} \\ = \text{be referred to as} \end{cases}$$

$$\begin{cases} = \text{be considered (to be)} \\ = \text{be thought (to be)} \end{cases}$$

故選 (B)。

If you're traveling abroad, don't let gift-giving customs <u>trip</u>
9

you <u>up</u>. Find out about the etiquette in the country you'll be
9

visiting. The right gift, given in the right way, can go a long

way toward <u>strengthening</u> new friendships.
10

如果你要到國外旅遊，不要讓送禮的習俗使你犯錯。要了解你要拜訪
的國家關於送禮的禮儀。適合的禮物，而且用適當的方法送，對強化
新的友誼大有幫助。

> ** abroad〔ə'brɔd〕*adv.* 到國外
>
> gift-giving〔'gɪft'gɪvɪŋ〕*adj.* 送禮物的
>
> custom〔'kʌstəm〕*n.* 習俗
>
> ***find out about*** 查明關於…的事實
>
> ***go a long way toward + V-ing*** 對…大有幫助

9. (**A**) 依句意，選 (A) ***trip sb. up*** 「使某人犯錯」。而 (B) trick
〔trɪk〕*v.* 欺騙【不加 on】，(C) burn down 「燒毀」，
(D) lay off 「暫時解雇」，用法與句意均不合。

10. (**D**) go a long way to 「對…大有用處」中的 to 是介系詞，其
後須接名詞或動名詞，故 (A) build 「建造」，(B) cement
〔sə'mɛnt〕*v.* 塗水泥於…；鞏固，用法不合；依句意選 (D)
strengthening。
strengthen〔'strɛŋθən〕*v.* 加強；使堅固
而 (C) interact〔‚ɪntə'ækt〕*v.* 相互作用；相互影響，
則不合句意。

TEST 36

Read the following passage and choose the best answer for each blank from the choices below.

Trying foods from other countries is a great way to experience different cultures and __1__ your horizons. Taipei restaurants offer not only Chinese food, but many delicious ethnic foods __2__. For example, when you visit an Italian restaurant, order a pasta dish, which usually __3__ a deliciously flavored tomato or cream sauce. Various kinds of cheeses also __4__ many Italian recipes. When __5__ at a Greek restaurant, don't forget Greek appetizers.

1. (A) broad   (B) extend   (C) expand   (D) explore

2. (A) as well   (B) as well as
   (C) so as well   (D) well as to

3. (A) comes by   (B) comes with
   (C) served as   (D) serving for

4. (A) compliment   (B) concern
   (C) complement   (D) complain

5. (A) dine   (B) to dine   (C) dining   (D) dined

The Greeks make many ___6___ dips, which are eaten with pita bread. The ___7___ of Mexican food is the tortilla, which tastes great with some hot sauce. Thai dishes are ___8___ visually appealing and flavorful, so before ___9___ a Thai dish, remember to note its color and presentation. India is the land of curries, strong flavors and powerful ___10___. You can finish the meal with Indian-style milk tea. 【延平高中】

6. (A) reckless   (B) cranky
    (C) heedless   (D) savory

7. (A) exterior   (B) mainstay
    (C) mainstream   (D) outlook

8. (A) in for   (B) meant to be
    (C) obliged to be   (D) in place of

9. (A) taking on   (B) trying on
    (C) dumpling   (D) sampling

10. (A) trinkets   (B) bonnets
    (C) aromas   (D) bicker

TEST 36 詳解

　　Trying foods from other countries is a great way to experience different cultures and <u>expand</u> your horizons.　Taipei
1

restaurants offer not only Chinese food, but many delicious ethnic foods <u>as well</u>.
2

　　嘗試其他國家的食物，是體驗不同文化，以及拓展眼界的絕佳方法。台北的餐廳不只提供中國菜，還有各民族的美味佳餚。

　　** experience〔ɪk'spɪrɪəns〕*v.* 體驗
　　　　horizons〔hə'raɪznz〕*n. pl.* 知識範圍；眼界
　　　　***not only…but (also)*~** 不僅…而且~
　　　　ethnic〔'ɛθnɪk〕*adj.* 民族特有的

1. (**C**)　依句意，「拓展」眼界，選 (C) ***expand***〔ɪk'spænd〕*v.* 擴大；
　　　　　展開。而 (A) broad〔brɔd〕*adj.* 寬廣的，要改成 broaden
　　　　　〔'brɔdn〕*v.* 使變寬；增廣 (見聞等)，(B) extend〔ɪk'stɛnd〕
　　　　　v. 延長，(D) explore〔ɪk'splor〕*v.* 探險；探索，不合句意。

2. (**A**)　依句意，選 (A) ***as well***「也」 (= *too*)。而 (B) as well as
　　　　　「以及」，則不合句意。

　　For example, when you visit an Italian restaurant, order a pasta dish, which usually <u>comes with</u> a deliciously flavored tomato
3

or cream sauce.　Various kinds of cheeses also <u>complement</u>
4

many Italian recipes.

例如，當你光臨義大利餐廳，點一道義大利麵，通常會附有風味可口的蕃茄醬，或奶油白醬。各式各樣的乳酪，也常被用來搭配許多義大利菜。

** visit〔'vɪzɪt〕 *v.* 去　　Italian〔ɪ'tæljən〕 *adj.* 義大利的
pasta〔'pɑstə〕 *n.* 麵食
deliciously〔dɪ'lɪʃəslɪ〕 *adv.* 美味地
flavored〔'flevəd〕 *adj.* 有…味的；風味…的
tomato〔tə'meto〕 *n.* 蕃茄　　sauce〔sɔs〕 *n.* 醬料
cream sauce 奶油白醬　　cheese〔tʃiz〕 *n.* 起司；乳酪
recipe〔'rɛsəpɪ〕 *n.* 食譜；烹飪法

3. (**B**)　依句意，選 (B) *comes with*「附有」。而 (A) come by「獲得」，(C) serve as「充當；擔任」，(D) serve for「用作；作爲」，則不合句意。

4. (**C**)　(A) compliment〔'kɑmplə,mɛnt〕 *v.* 稱讚
(B) concern〔kən'sɜn〕 *v.* 與…有關
(C) *complement*〔'kɑmplə,mɛnt〕 *v.* 補充；與…搭配
(D) complain〔kəm'plen〕 *v.* 抱怨

When <u>dining</u> at a Greek restaurant, don't forget Greek
      5
appetizers.　The Greeks make many <u>savory</u> dips, which are
         6
eaten with pita bread.　The <u>mainstay</u> of Mexican food is the
       7
tortilla, which tastes great with some hot sauce.
在希臘餐廳吃飯時，別忘了希臘式開胃菜。希臘人會做很多種可口的醬汁，跟皮塔麵包一起食用。墨西哥菜的主軸，是墨西哥玉米餅，跟辣醬一起吃非常美味。

** Greek〔grik〕*adj.* 希臘的　*n.* 希臘人
　appetizer〔'æpə,taɪzɚ〕*n.* 開胃菜
　dip〔dɪp〕*n.* 調味醬汁
　pita〔'pitə〕*n.* 皮塔麵包【一種中東人食用的圓扁型麵包】
　pita bread 皮塔麵包 (= *pita*)
　Mexican〔'mɛksɪkən〕*adj.* 墨西哥的
　tortilla〔tɔr'tijɑ〕*n.* 墨西哥玉米餅　　*hot sauce* 辣醬

5. (**C**) 原句為：When you are dining at…，又副詞子句中，句
　　　意很明顯，主詞和 be 動詞可同時省略，故選 (C) *dining*。
　　　dine〔daɪn〕*v.* 用餐

6. (**D**) (A) reckless〔'rɛklɪs〕*adj.* 魯莽的
　　　(B) cranky〔'kræŋkɪ〕*adj.* 古怪的；難以取悅的
　　　(C) heedless〔'hidlɪs〕*adj.* 不注意的；漫不經心的
　　　(D) *savory*〔'sevərɪ〕*adj.* 可口的；有香味的

7. (**B**) 依句意，選 (B) *mainstay*〔'men,ste〕*n.* 主要的依靠；
　　　支柱；台柱。而 (A) exterior〔ɪk'stɪrɪɚ〕*n.* 外部，
　　　(C) mainstream〔'men,strim〕*n.* 主流；主要傾向，
　　　(D) outlook〔'aut,luk〕*n.* 看法，均不合句意。

Thai dishes are <u>meant to be</u> visually appealing and flavorful, so
　　　　　　　　　　8
before <u>sampling</u> a Thai dish, remember to note its color and
　　　　9
presentation.　India is the land of curries, strong flavors and
powerful <u>aromas</u>.　You can finish the meal with Indian-style
　　　　10
milk tea.

泰國菜會在視覺上非常吸引人，而且充滿香味，所以在吃泰國菜之前，記得留意菜的色澤和呈現的方式。印度是咖哩的國度，咖哩有濃濃的味道跟強烈的香氣。在用餐的最後，你可以用印度式奶茶作為結尾。

** Thai〔'tɑ‧i〕*adj.* 泰國的

visually〔'vɪʒʊəlɪ〕*adv.* 看起來；在外觀上

appealing〔ə'pilɪŋ〕*adj.* 吸引人的

flavorful〔'flevəfəl〕*adj.* 充滿香味的　　note〔not〕*v.* 注意

presentation〔ˌprɛzn̩'teʃən〕*n.* 外觀；呈現

India〔'ɪndɪə〕*n.* 印度　　land〔lænd〕*n.* 國家

curry〔'kɝɪ〕*n.* 咖哩　　flavor〔'flevə〕*n.* 味道；香味

powerful〔'paʊəfəl〕*adj.*（氣味）強烈的

meal〔mil〕*n.* 一餐

Indian-style〔'ɪndɪən'staɪl〕*adj.* 印度式的　　*milk tea* 奶茶

8.(**B**) 依句意，選 (B) *be meant to V*.「目的是為了～；打算要～」
（= *be designed to V.*）。而 (A) be in for「註定要遭受」，
(C) be obliged to V.「不得不～」，(D) be in place of「代
替」，則不合句意。

9.(**D**) 在「品嚐」泰國菜之前，選 (D) *sampling*。
sample〔'sæmpl̩〕*v.* 品嚐
而 (A) take on「承擔」，(B) try on「試穿」，(C) dumpling
〔'dʌmplɪŋ〕*n.* 水餃，皆不合句意。

10.(**C**) (A) trinket〔'trɪŋkɪt〕*n.* 小飾物
(B) bonnet〔'bɑnɪt〕*n.* 無邊軟帽
(C) *aroma*〔ə'romə〕*n.* 芳香；香味
(D) bicker〔'bɪkə〕*n. v.* 爭論；爭吵

TEST 37

*Read the following passage and choose the best answer for each
blank from the choices below.*

Many cities around the world are beginning to develop
recycling projects. These projects typically include strategies
for ___1___ waste, often by using waste ___2___ raw material
for building homes, generating energy, or cultivating crops,
for example. One effective waste-management program
can be found in Copenhagen, Denmark. ___3___ the impact
of the waste-management system, the Copenhagen City
Council ___4___ new laws in 1991, requiring that waste
producers separate all waste at the place of ___5___ .

1. (A) burying   (B) picking
   (C) reducing   (D) dumping

2. (A) as   (B) for   (C) with   (D) to

3. (A) To increasing   (B) Increasing
   (C) To increase   (D) Increased

4. (A) adapted (B) adept (C) adopted (D) adjusted

5. (A) product   (B) production
   (C) productivity   (D) produce

In addition, waste producers need to reduce the waste
___6___ to landfills by introducing new technologies,
processes, or recycling methods. ___7___ these
regulations, the number of landfills in use has been cut
from 30 to 3. Today more than 50 percent of the city's
commercial and industrial waste ___8___ recycled. ___9___,
about 50,000 tons of garbage, previously deposited in
landfills, are now transformed ___10___ energy. 【西松高中】

6. (A) sent   (B) sending
   (C) send   (D) that sent

7. (A) Resulted in   (B) As a result of
   (C) Because   (D) Contribute to

8. (A) is   (B) be
   (C) are   (D) being

9. (A) Furthermore   (B) Beside
   (C) In addition to   (D) What's worse

10. (A) from   (B) at
    (C) with   (D) into

TEST 37 詳解

Many cities around the world are beginning to develop recycling projects. These projects typically include strategies for reducing waste, often by using waste as raw material for
　　　　　1　　　　　　　　　　　　　　　　2
building homes, generating energy, or cultivating crops, for example.

全世界許多城市，都開始研發資源回收計畫。這些計畫通常包含減少廢棄物的方法，例如經常把廢棄物拿來當蓋房子的原料、產生能源，或是栽培農作物。

** develop〔dɪ'vɛləp〕*v.* 研發
　　recycling〔ri'saɪklɪŋ〕*n.* 資源回收
　　project〔'prɑdʒɛkt〕*n.* 計畫
　　typically〔'tɪpɪkḷɪ〕*adv.* 通常
　　strategy〔'strætədʒɪ〕*n.* 策略；方法
　　waste〔west〕*n.* 廢棄物；垃圾
　　raw〔rɔ〕*adj.* 未加工的　　***raw material*** 原料
　　generate〔'dʒɛnəˌret〕*v.* 產生　　energy〔'ɛnədʒɪ〕*n.* 能源
　　cultivate〔'kʌltəˌvet〕*v.* 栽培　　crop〔krɑp〕*n.* 農作物

1. (**C**) 依句意，選 (C) *reducing*「減少」。而 (A) bury〔'bɛrɪ〕*v.* 埋藏，(B) pick〔pɪk〕*v.* 摘；挖，(D) dump〔dʌmp〕*v.* 傾倒，均不合句意。

2. (**A**) *use* A *as* B　把 A 當作 B 來使用

One effective waste-management program can be found in
Copenhagen, Denmark. <u>To increase</u> the impact of the
 3
waste-management system, the Copenhagen City Council
<u>adopted</u> new laws in 1991, requiring that waste producers
 4
separate all waste at the place of <u>production</u>.
 5

在丹麥首都哥本哈根，有一種有效的廢棄物管理計劃。為了增加
廢棄物管理系統的成效，哥本哈根市議會在 1991 年採用新的法
律，要求垃圾製造者，在製造垃圾的地點就要做好垃圾分類。

> ** effective〔ɪˋfɛktɪv〕*adj.* 有效的
> management〔ˋmænɪdʒmənt〕*n.* 管理
> waste-management〔ˋwestˋmænɪdʒmənt〕*adj.* 廢棄物管理的
> program〔ˋprogræm〕*n.* 計畫
> Copenhagen〔͵kopənˋhegən〕*n.* 哥本哈根【丹麥首都】
> Denmark〔ˋdɛnmark〕*n.* 丹麥【北歐國家】
> impact〔ˋɪmpækt〕*n.* 影響；效果
> council〔ˋkaʊnsḷ〕*n.* 議會　　require〔rɪˋkwaɪr〕*v.* 要求
> producer〔prəˋdjusɚ〕*n.* 製造者
> separate〔ˋsɛpə͵ret〕*v.* 把⋯分開；區別

3. (**C**) 表「目的」，須用不定詞，故選 (C) ***To increase***「為了
　　　增加」。

4. (**C**) 依句意，「採用」新法律，選 (C) ***adopted***。而 (A)
　　　adapt〔əˋdæpt〕*v.* 適應；改編，(B) adept〔əˋdɛpt〕
　　　adj. 精通的，(D) adjust〔əˋdʒʌst〕*v.* 調整，均不合
　　　句意。

5. (**B**) 依句意，要求垃圾的製造者，在「製造」垃圾的地點就
要將垃圾分類，選 (B) *production* 〔 prəˈdʌkʃən 〕 *n.* 生
產；製造。而 (A) product「產品」，(C) productivity
〔ˌprodʌkˈtɪvətɪ 〕 *n.* 生產力，(D) produce 〔 prəˈdjus 〕
v. 生產；製造；〔ˈprɑdjus 〕 *n.* 農產品，均不合句意。

In addition, waste producers need to reduce the waste <u>sent</u>
6

to landfills by introducing new technologies, processes, or
recycling methods.
此外，垃圾製造者必須引進新的技術、程序，或回收的方法，來減
少運往垃圾掩埋場的垃圾量。

> ** *in addition* 此外 　　landfill 〔ˈlændˌfɪl 〕 *n.* 垃圾掩埋場
> introduce 〔ˌɪntrəˈdjus 〕 *v.* 引進
> technology 〔 tɛkˈnɑlədʒɪ 〕 *n.* 科技
> process 〔ˈprɑsɛs 〕 *n.* 過程；方法
> method 〔ˈmɛθəd 〕 *n.* 方法

6. (**A**) 依句意，「被送往」掩埋場的垃圾，須用被動語態，故
選 (A) *sent*。本句是由…the waste *which is* sent…簡
化而來。

<u>As a result of</u> these regulations, the number of landfills in use
7

has been cut from 30 to 3.　Today more than 50 percent of the
city's commercial and industrial waste <u>is</u> recycled.
8

因為有這些規定，讓使用中的垃圾掩埋場，從三十個減少到三個。
現在該城市百分之五十以上的商業和工業廢棄物都可以被回收。

** regulation〔͵rɛgjə'leʃən〕*n.* 規定　　***in use*** 使用中的
cut〔kʌt〕*v.* 減少　　commercial〔kə'mɝʃəl〕*adj.* 商業的
industrial〔ɪn'dʌstrɪəl〕*adj.* 工業的
recycle〔ri'saɪkl̩〕*v.* 回收再利用

7.(**B**)　依句意,「因為」這些規定,且空格後是名詞,不可用連
接詞 Because,故選 (B) ***As a result of***「因為;由於」。
而 (A) result in「導致」,(D) contribute to「促成;有
助於」,用法與句意皆不合。

8.(**A**)　waste 為不可數名詞,所以主詞 more than 50 percent
of the city's commercial and industrial waste 視為單
數,且依句意為現在式,故選 (A) ***is***。

Furthermore, about 50,000 tons of garbage, previously
　　9
deposited in landfills, are now transformed into energy.
　　　　　　　　　　　　　　　　　　　　　　10
此外,之前堆在垃圾掩埋場大約五萬公噸的垃圾,現在已經被轉
化成能源了。

** ton〔tʌn〕*n.* 公噸　　previously〔'privɪəslɪ〕*adv.* 之前
deposit〔dɪ'pɑzɪt〕*v.* 放置
transform〔træns'fɔrm〕*v.* 使轉變

9.(**A**)　依句意,選 (A) ***Furthermore***「此外」。而 (B) beside「在
～旁邊」,須改為 besides「此外」才能選;(C) in addition
to「除了…之外(還有)」,後須接名詞,用法與句意皆
不合;(D) what's worse「更糟的是」,則不合句意。

10.(**D**)　***be transformed into*** 被轉變成

TEST 38

Read the following passage and choose the best answer for each blank from the choices below.

Everyone is the pilot of his life. However, people who really take good control of their lives are those who ___1___ for their own actions. When something needs ___2___, instead of ___3___ a mysterious person ___4___ Somebody Else, they always decide to respond immediately. Never do they wait until the situation is ___5___. The inner cry they hear is not "What will Somebody Else do for me?" but "What will I do?"

1. (A) takes full responsibility
   (B) are fully responsible
   (C) are fully irresponsible
   (D) takes over their responsibility

2. (A) do   (B) to do
   (C) to be done   (D) to be doing

3. (A) count on   (B) relying on
   (C) depending   (D) dependency on

4. (A) refer to   (B) referring to
   (C) referring to as   (D) referred to as

5. (A) under control   (B) losing control
   (C) out of control   (D) not in control

Shirley M. Dever is a good example. When a paraplegic girl requested financial aid to go to Hawaii, Shirley, in response to the ___6___, made sixty phone calls right away ___7___. Amazingly, within a week, thirty-eight people sent her checks ___8___ one thousand dollars, ___9___ the girl to realize her dream. Many Somebody Elses helped Shirley, ___10___, but it was Shirley's immediate actions that got the great job done. The girl fulfilled her dream of seeing Hawaii, and Shirley fulfilled her goal of being Somebody in someone else's life. 【內湖高中】

6. (A) duty　　(B) plea　　(C) misery　　(D) plead

7. (A) on the behalf　　　　(B) for the behalf
　　(C) for behalf　　　　　(D) on her behalf

8. (A) totaled　　　　　　　(B) total
　　(C) which total　　　　　(D) totaling

9. (A) which helped　　　　(B) helped
　　(C) help　　　　　　　　(D) it helped

10. (A) to do her justice　　(B) to make it short
　　 (C) to be sure　　　　　(D) to begin with

TEST 38 詳解

Everyone is the pilot of his life. However, people who really take good control of their lives are those who <u>are fully responsible</u> for their own actions.
　　　　1

　　每個人都是自己生命的領航者。然而，眞正能夠好好掌控自己生活的人，是那些能對自己的行爲全權負責的人。

** pilot〔ˈpaɪlət〕*n.* 駕駛員；領航員
take control of 控制　　action〔ˈækʃən〕*n.* 行動

1.(**B**)　依句意，是能「對」自己的行爲「全權負責」的人，又主詞
　　　　those 是複數形，所以 (A) takes full responsibility「負全
　　　　責」，(D) takes over their responsibility「接管他們的責
　　　　任」，用法不合；而 (C) are fully irresponsible「完全不
　　　　負責任」，則不合句意，故選 (B) *are fully responsible*。

When something needs <u>to be done</u>, instead of <u>relying on</u> a
　　　　　　　　　　2　　　　　　　　3
mysterious person <u>referred to as</u> Somebody Else, they always
　　　　　　　　4
decide to respond immediately. Never do they wait until the
situation is <u>out of control</u>. The inner cry they hear is not
　　　　　　　5
"What will Somebody Else do for me?" but "What will I do?"
當需要做某件事情的時候，他們不會依賴被稱爲「他者」的神秘之人，
而總是會決定要立刻做出回應，他們絕不會等到事情變得無法收拾。
他們內心聽到的聲音不是「別人能爲我做什麼？」而是「我能夠做些
什麼？」

** ***instead of*** 而非…   mysterious〔mɪsˈtɪrɪəs〕*adj.* 神秘的
Somebody Else 他者【在心理學跟社會學中,所謂的「他者」
是指在自己生命中出現,具有特殊意義的人,如家人、老師、
朋友等,甚至是在你有需要時伸出援手的陌生人】
respond〔rɪˈspɑnd〕*v.* 回應
immediately〔ɪˈmidɪɪtlɪ〕*adv.* 立刻
situation〔ˌsɪtʃʊˈeʃən〕*n.* 情況
inner〔ˈɪnɚ〕*adj.* 內在的   cry〔kraɪ〕*n.* 叫聲;吶喊
not A ***but*** B 不是 A,而是 B

2.(**C**) 事情需要「被做」,故選 (C)***to be done***。

3.(**B**) of 為介系詞,其後須接名詞或動名詞,依句意,選 (B)
relying on「依賴」。

$$\left\{ \begin{array}{l} \text{rely on 依賴} \\ = \text{count on} \\ = \text{depend on} \end{array} \right.$$

(D) dependency on「對…的依賴」,則不合句意。

4.(**D**) 依句意,是被稱為他者的人,空格應填 who is referred to
as,又關代 who 和 be 動詞 is 可同時省略,故選 (D)
referred to as。
be referred to as 被稱為

5.(**C**) 依句意,選 (C)***be out of control***「失去控制」。而 (A) be
under control「受控制」,(B) be losing control「正在
失控」,(D) be not in control「沒有在掌控」,皆不合句
意。

Shirley M. Dever is a good example.　When a paraplegic
girl requested financial aid to go to Hawaii, Shirley, in response
to the <u>plea</u>, made sixty phone calls right away <u>on her behalf</u>.
　　　　 6　　　　　　　　　　　　　　　　　　　　　　　　 7
　　雪莉・M・迪佛是個很好的例子。當一位下半身癱瘓的女孩，向
她要求去夏威夷的金錢援助時，雪莉為了回應這項請求，馬上替她撥
打六十通電話。

　　** paraplegic〔͵pærə′plɪdʒɪk〕*adj.* 下半身癱瘓的
　　　　request〔rɪ′kwɛst〕*v.* 要求
　　　　financial〔fə′nænʃəl〕*adj.* 財務的
　　　　aid〔ed〕*n.* 援助　　***in response to*** 為了回應
　　　make a phone call 打電話　　***right away*** 立刻

6. (**B**)　(A) duty〔′djutɪ〕*n.* 責任
　　　　　(B) ***plea***〔pli〕*n.* 懇求
　　　　　(C) misery〔′mɪzərɪ〕*n.* 悲慘；不幸
　　　　　(D) plead〔plid〕*v.* 為⋯辯護

7. (**D**)　***on one's behalf*** 代表某人 (*= on behalf of sb.*)

Amazingly, within a week, thirty-eight people sent her checks
<u>totaling</u> one thousand dollars, <u>which helped</u> the girl to realize
　 8　　　　　　　　　　　　　　　　　 9
her dream.
令人驚奇的是，在一週內，有三十八個人，寄來總計一千元美金的支
票給雪莉，幫助那個女孩實現她的夢想。

　　** amazingly〔ə′mezɪŋlɪ〕*adv.* 驚人地
　　　　check〔tʃɛk〕*n.* 支票　　realize〔′rɪə͵laɪz〕*v.* 實現

8. (**D**) 支票「總共」一千元美金，且依句意為過去式，故空格應填 which totaled，又關代 which 可省略，但動詞須改為現在分詞，故選 (D) *totaling*。

total〔'totḷ〕*v.* 總計；共計

9. (**A**) 空格應填關代，引導形容詞子句，修飾先行詞 checks，故選 (A) *which helped*。而 (B) 須改為 helping 才能選。

Many Somebody Elses helped Shirley, <u>to be sure</u>, but it was
                                              10
Shirley's immediate actions that got the great job done. The
girl fulfilled her dream of seeing Hawaii, and Shirley fulfilled
her goal of being Somebody in someone else's life.

的確很多所謂的「他者」幫助了雪莉，但其實是因為雪莉立即的行動，才完成這項艱鉅的任務。那個女孩實現了遊覽夏威夷的夢想，而雪莉也達成目標，在別人的生命中當個重要的人。

** immediate〔ɪ'midɪɪt〕*adj.* 立即的

job〔dʒɑb〕*n.* 工作；任務；很艱難的事

fulfill〔fʊl'fɪl〕*v.* 完成；達成　　goal〔gol〕*n.* 目標

somebody〔'sʌm,bɑdɪ〕*n.* 某人；重要人物

10. (**C**)　(A) to do *one* justice　平心而論

(B) to make it short　長話短說（= *to make a long story short*）

(C) *to be sure*　的確；當然

~, *to be sure, but*…　的確~，但是…

(D) to begin with　首先

TEST 39

Read the following passage and choose the best answer for each blank from the choices below.

When it comes ___1___, Norman Vincent Peale was an expert. When ___2___ the church feud between Mrs. Lloyd and Mrs. Follet, he started his magic by telling Mrs. Follet that her opponent said she was a good cook. ___3___, she managed to compliment Peggy Lloyd on her pastry making. Surprisingly, that little flicker of goodwill ___4___ solving the problem.

1. (A) to give compliments
   (B) to giving compliments
   (C) to compliment   (D) to give compliment

2. (A) confronting   (B) facing with
   (C) faced   (D) confronted

3. (A) Reluctant as she was
   (B) Reluctant being
   (C) Reluctant as she showed
   (D) Reluctant although she was

4. (A) ended up as   (B) ended up to
   (C) ended up   (D) ended up to be

For each person in the parish, it was a relief no longer

____5____ to take sides. Did Dr. Peale find ____6____ difficult

to be the man in the middle? Actually, he didn't. ____7____

was listen for words of approval and pass them along. The

recipient felt ____8____ the effort he made and he/she certainly

benefited ____9____ the love and power in praise. In a word,

we human beings all have the need to be appreciated. If you

find any chance to let others know how much they are loved,

don't hesitate! It's 100 percent ____10____! 【板橋高中】

5. (A) have   (B) had   (C) has   (D) having

6. (A) which   (B) that   (C) what   (D) it

7. (A) Whatever he does   (B) However he does
   (C) All that he does   (D) Everything he does

8. (A) grateful for   (B) thankful to
   (C) grateful to   (D) appreciative for

9. (A) within   (B) for   (C) from   (D) towards

10. (A) awarding   (B) award
    (C) reward   (D) rewarding

TEST 39 詳解

When it comes <u>to giving compliments</u>, Norman Vincent
1

Peale was an expert.

一提到讚美別人，諾曼・文森・皮爾先生是個專家。

** ***when it comes to*** 一提到
　　expert〔'εkspɜt〕*n.* 專家

1. (**B**)　When it comes to「一提到」中的 to 是介系詞，其後須接
　　　　　　動名詞，故選 (B) ***to giving compliments***「給別人讚美」。
　　　　　　compliment〔'kɑmpləmənt〕*n.* 稱讚

When <u>confronting</u> the church feud between Mrs. Lloyd and Mrs.
2

Follet, he started his magic by telling Mrs. Follet that her

opponent said she was a good cook.　<u>Reluctant as she was</u>, she
3

managed to compliment Peggy Lloyd on her pastry making.

當他面對教會中洛伊德太太跟法洛太太彼此仇視時，他展開他的魔法，
告訴法洛太太說，她的對手說她很會做菜。雖然法洛太太很不情願，但
還是設法讚美珮姬・洛伊德的糕餅做得很好。

** feud〔fjud〕*n.* 宿仇；不合
　　start〔stɑrt〕*v.* 開始；啟動　　magic〔'mædʒɪk〕*n.* 魔法
　　opponent〔ə'ponənt〕*n.* 對手
　　cook〔kʊk〕*n.* 廚師　　manage〔'mænɪdʒ〕*v.* 設法
　　compliment〔'kɑmplə‚mɛnt〕*v.* 稱讚
　　pastry〔'pestrɪ〕*n.* 糕餅

2. (**A**) 「當他面對…」的說法有：

> When he faced…
> = When he was faced with…
> = When he confronted…
> = When he was confronted with…

可簡化為：

> When facing…
> = When faced with…
> = When *confronting*…
> = When confronted with…　　故選 (A)。

3. (**A**) 「雖然她很不情願」的說法有：

> *Although* she was reluctant…
> = Reluctant *as/though* she was…　　故選 (A)。

而 (C) show「顯現；表現」，為及物動詞，在此用法不合。

Surprisingly, that little flicker of goodwill <u>ended up</u> solving the
4
problem. For each person in the parish, it was a relief no longer
<u>having</u> to take sides.
5

令人驚訝的是，這些突然顯現的一點善意，最後解決了問題。對於教區
內的每個人來說，不用再選邊站，真是鬆了一口氣。

> ** surprisingly〔 sə'praɪzɪŋlɪ 〕*adv.* 令人驚訝的是
> flicker〔'flɪkə 〕*n.* 閃現；突然而短暫的動作
> goodwill〔'gʊd'wɪl 〕*n.* 善意　　solve〔 sɑlv 〕*v.* 解決
> parish〔'pærɪʃ 〕*n.* 教區
> relief〔 rɪ'lif 〕*n.* 解除；放心；鬆了一口氣
> *no longer* 不再　　*take sides* 選邊站

4. (**C**) ***end up + V-ing***　結果～；最後～

　　　而 (A)「end up as + 身份」，表「最後成為～」，在此不合。

5. (**D**) it 為虛主詞，故空格應填真正主詞，故須用動名詞 ***having***，
　　　選 (D)。

Did Dr. Peale find <u>it</u> difficult to be the man in the middle?
　　　　　　　　　　6

Actually, he didn't.　<u>All that he did</u> was listen for words of
　　　　　　　　　　　　　　　7

approval and pass them along.　The recipient felt <u>grateful for</u> the
　　　　　　　　　　　　　　　　　　　　　　　　　　8

effort he made and he/she certainly benefited <u>from</u> the love and
　　　　　　　　　　　　　　　　　　　　　　9

power in praise.

皮爾博士覺得做個中間人很困難嗎？其實他不這麼覺得。他所做的，
就只是仔細聽一些贊同的話，然後再把話傳出去。受到讚美的人很感
激他所做的努力，而且也一定能從讚美的愛與力量中獲益。

　　** find〔faɪnd〕*v.* 覺得　　***in the middle***　夾在中間
　　　actually〔'æktʃʊəlɪ〕*adv.* 事實上　　***listen for***　專注傾聽
　　　approval〔ə'pruvl̩〕*n.* 贊同；肯定　　***pass along***　傳遞
　　　recipient〔rɪ'sɪpɪənt〕*n.* 接受者　　***make efforts***　努力
　　　certainly〔'sɝtn̩lɪ〕*adv.* 必定　　benefit〔'bɛnəfɪt〕*v.* 獲益
　　　praise〔prez〕*n.* 讚美

6. (**D**) 空格應填虛受詞，代替真正受詞 to be the man in the
　　　middle，故選 (D) ***it***。

7. (**C**) 依句意，選 (C) ***All that he did***。
　　　all that one does is + (to) ***V.***　某人所做的就是…

8. (**A**)　表「對某事覺得感激」的說法有：

> be thankful *for sth.*
> = be grateful *for sth.*
> = be appreciative *of sth.*　故選 (A)。

而 (B) be thankful to 及 (C) be grateful to 都須加「人」，
表「感激某人」，在此用法不合。

grateful〔'gretfəl〕*adj.* 感激的
appreciative〔ə'priʃɪ,etɪv〕*adj.* 感激的

9. (**C**)　表「從…中」獲益，介系詞須用 ***from***，選 (C)。

In a word, we human beings all have the need to be appreciated.
If you find any chance to let others know how much they are
loved, don't hesitate!　It's 100 percent <u>rewarding</u>!
　　　　　　　　　　　　　　　　　10

總之，我們人類都有被欣賞的需求。如果你有機會讓其他人知道，自
己有多麼受人喜愛，那就不要猶豫！這樣做是百分之百有好處的！

> ** ***in a word*** 總之　　***human beings*** 人類
> 　 appreciate〔ə'priʃɪ,et〕*v.* 欣賞
> 　 hesitate〔'hɛzə,tet〕*v.* 猶豫
> 　 percent〔pɚ'sɛnt〕*n.* 百分之…

10. (**D**)　空格應填形容詞，且依句意，選 (D) ***rewarding***〔rɪ'wɔrdɪŋ〕
　　　　　adj. 值得做的；有益的。而 (B) award〔ə'wɔrd〕*n.* 獎
　　　　　v. 頒發，(C) reward〔rɪ'wɔrd〕*n.* 報酬；獎賞　*v.* 酬謝，
　　　　　用法與句意均不合。

TEST 40

Read the following passage and choose the best answer for each blank from the choices below.

A Roman poet once said, "Pygmies placed on the shoulders of giants see more than the giants themselves." Indeed, some great minds in history have had a positive and long-lasting ___1___ on mankind. Without them, human civilization would never have been developed. Among these influential people, Confucius is the one whose teachings have guided billions of Chinese.

___2___ in writings called Analects, Confucius' teachings represent the basic tenets of Chinese thought.

1. (A) effect   (B) gravity
   (C) explanations   (D) awareness

2. (A) When been preserved
   (B) To be preserved
   (C) Preserving   (D) Preserved

As ___3___ as Eastern Confucianism, Christianity has long led the ideology of the west. Jesus Christ taught people to have a relationship with God and also urged people to love one another. Isaac Newton was another passionate figure, eager to know how God's universe worked. His ___4___ the truth of the universe led to many modern discoveries. It was he that revolutionized science ___5___ explaining the physical world in mathematical terms. Undoubtedly, these great lives prove that one person can change the whole world.

【師大附中】

3. (A) earnest   (B) profound
   (C) luxurious   (D) narrow

4. (A) ignorance of   (B) battle against
   (C) quest for   (D) popularity with

5. (A) by   (B) with
   (C) in   (D) from

TEST　40　詳解

A Roman poet once said, "Pygmies placed on the shoulders of giants see more than the giants themselves." Indeed, some great minds in history have had a positive and long-lasting <u>effect</u> on mankind. Without them, human civilization would
　1
never have been developed.

　　有個羅馬詩人曾說過：「將俾格米人放在巨人的肩膀上，他將比巨人看得更多更廣。」的確，歷史上某些偉人，對全人類有著正面且長遠的影響。沒有他們，就無法發展人類文明。

　** Roman〔'romən〕*adj.* 羅馬的　　poet〔'po‧ɪt〕*n.* 詩人
　　　pygmy〔'pɪgmɪ〕*n.* 俾格米人（赤道附近的矮黑人）；侏儒
　　　place〔ples〕*v.* 放置　　giant〔'dʒaɪənt〕*n.* 巨人
　　　Pygmies placed on the shoulders of giants see more than
　　　　the giants themselves. 將俾格米人放在巨人肩膀上，他將
　　　　比巨人看得更多更廣。【本句出自馬庫斯‧盧肯（Marcus Lucan,
　　　　39-65 A.D.）之名言，意思為做學問時，要以古人所打下的基礎為
　　　　根基，如此才能有更偉大的成就】
　　　indeed〔ɪn'did〕*adv.* 的確　　***great mind*** 偉人
　　　positive〔'pɑzətɪv〕*adj.* 正面的
　　　long-lasting〔'lɔŋ'læstɪŋ〕*adj.* 持久的
　　　mankind〔mæn'kaɪnd〕*n.* 人類
　　　civilization〔ˌsɪvḷə'zeʃən〕*n.* 文明

1.（**A**）　(A) ***effect***〔ɪ'fɛkt〕*n.* 影響
　　　　　(B) gravity〔'grævətɪ〕*n.* 重力；地心引力
　　　　　(C) explanation〔ˌɛksplə'neʃən〕*n.* 解釋
　　　　　(D) awareness〔ə'wɛrnɪs〕*n.* 察覺；意識

Among these influential people, Confucius is the one whose teachings have guided billions of Chinese. <u>Preserved</u> in

2

writings called Analects, Confucius' teachings represent the basic tenets of Chinese thought.

在這些有影響力的人當中，孔子的學說指引了數十億中國人。孔子的學說代表著中國思想的基本教條，被收錄在「論語」這本著作當中。

** influential〔͵ɪnflʊ'ɛnʃəl〕*adj.* 有影響力的

Confucius〔kən'fjuʃəs〕*n.* 孔子【約 551-479B.C.，儒家思想始祖】

teachings〔'titʃɪŋz〕*n. pl.* 教訓；學說

guide〔gaɪd〕*v.* 引導　　billion〔'bɪljən〕*n.* 十億

writings〔'raɪtɪŋz〕*n. pl.* 著作；作品

analects〔'ænə͵lɛkts〕*n. pl.* 語錄；文選【*the Analects of Confucius* 論語】

represent〔͵rɛprɪ'zɛnt〕*v.* 代表

tenet〔'tɛnɪt〕*n.* 主義；教義

2.(**D**) 原句為：Confucius' teachings are preserved in writings⋯, and they represent basic⋯。因為分詞構句可代替第一個對等子句，但須放在主詞前面，故可簡化為：Preserved in⋯, Confucius' teachings are⋯。【詳見「文法寶典」p.459】

As <u>profound</u> as Eastern Confucianism, Christianity has long

3

led the ideology of the west. Jesus Christ taught people to have a relationship with God and also urged people to love one another.

基督教教義和東方的儒家思想一樣深奧，長久以來引領西方世界的
意識形態。耶穌基督教導人民如何和上帝產生連結，並且勸導人們
要相親相愛。

   ** eastern〔'istən〕*adj.* 東方的
       Confucianism〔kən'fjuʃən,ɪzəm〕*n.* 孔子思想；儒家思想
       Christianity〔,krɪstʃɪ'ænətɪ〕*n.* 基督教；基督教教義
       ideology〔,aɪdɪ'alədʒɪ〕*n.* 意識形態
       Jesus Christ〔'dʒizəs'kraɪst〕*n.* 耶穌基督
       have a relationship with　和⋯有關係；和⋯產生交流
       urge〔ɝdʒ〕*v.* 催促；力勸

3. (**B**)　(A) earnest〔'ɝnɪst〕*adj.* 認真的；誠摯的
     (B) ***profound***〔prə'faʊnd〕*adj.* 深奧的；深遠的
     (C) luxurious〔lʌg'ʒʊrɪəs〕*adj.* 奢侈的；豪華的
     (D) narrow〔'næro〕*adj.* 狹窄的；勉強的

Isaac Newton was another passionate figure, eager to know
how God's universe worked. His quest for the truth of the
                                 4
universe led to many modern discoveries. It was he that
revolutionized science by explaining the physical world in
                              5
mathematical terms.
艾薩克・牛頓是另一個充滿熱情的人物，他渴望知道上帝的世界是如
何運作的。他對宇宙真理的追求造成許多現代的發現。就是牛頓藉由
用數學名詞解釋自然界，使科學有了革命性的變化。

** Isaac Newton〔'aɪzək'njutṇ〕n. 艾薩克・牛頓【1642-1729，
英國物理學家、數學家，發明微積分，發現萬有引力以及三大
運動定律。他曾説過：「如果我看得更遠，是因為我站在巨人
的肩膀上。」表示自己對先前科學家的推崇跟景仰】

passionate〔'pæʃənɪt〕adj. 熱情的
figure〔'fɪgjɚ〕n. 人物　　**be eager to** + **V.** 渴望
universe〔'junəˌvɝs〕n. 宇宙　　work〔wɝk〕v. 運作
lead to 導致　　　discovery〔dɪ'skʌvərɪ〕n. 發現
revolutionize〔ˌrɛvə'luʃənˌaɪz〕v. 革命；徹底改革
physical〔'fɪzɪkḷ〕adj. 自然界的；物理的
mathematical〔ˌmæθə'mætɪkḷ〕adj. 數學的
term〔tɝm〕n. 名詞；用語

4. (**C**)　依句意，選 (C) **quest for**「對～的追求」。

quest〔kwɛst〕n. 追求
而 (A) ignorance of「對～的無知」，(B) battle against
「對抗～的戰役」，(D) popularity with「受～的歡迎」，
則不合句意。

5. (**A**)　表「藉由～」，介系詞用 **by**，選 (A)。

Undoubtedly, these great lives prove that one person can change
the whole world.

無疑地，這些偉大的人證明，一個人也能改變全世界。

** undoubtedly〔ʌn'daʊtɪdlɪ〕adv. 無疑地
life〔laɪf〕n.（有生命的）人
prove〔pruv〕v. 證明

本書答題錯誤率分析表

本資料經過「劉毅英文家教班」克漏字測驗大賽391多位同學實際考試過，經過電腦統計分析，錯誤率如下：

測 驗	題號	正確選項	錯誤率	最多人選的錯誤選項	測 驗	題號	正確選項	錯誤率	最多人選的錯誤選項
Test 1	1	B	43 %	A	Test 13	1	C	26 %	D
	2	A	22 %	D		2	A	72 %	B
	3	B	88 %	A		3	C	33 %	B
	4	D	51 %	A		4	B	27 %	A
	5	A	62 %	B		5	C	57 %	A
Test 2	1	D	47 %	B		6	A	33 %	D
	2	D	56 %	B		7	B	60 %	A
	3	C	30 %	D		8	C	59 %	A
	4	A	51 %	C		9	C	60 %	B
	5	A	28 %	B		10	A	69 %	D
Test 3	1	C	34 %	D	Test 14	1	A	42 %	B
	2	B	23 %	D		2	D	42 %	B
	3	B	25 %	C		3	B	39 %	D
	4	C	17 %	D		4	D	31 %	A
	5	A	32 %	C		5	D	39 %	C
Test 4	1	C	56 %	A	Test 15	1	B	61 %	A
	2	A	39 %	B		2	C	20 %	D
	3	C	40 %	A		3	D	34 %	B
	4	D	48 %	B		4	B	57 %	A
	5	D	95 %	B		5	B	55 %	D
Test 5	1	C	18 %	A	Test 16	1	A	23 %	B
	2	B	25 %	A		2	B	45 %	C
	3	D	48 %	A		3	C	18 %	B
	4	B	61 %	D		4	D	24 %	B
	5	A	22 %	C		5	A	43 %	B
Test 6	1	D	21 %	A	Test 17	1	A	51 %	D
	2	D	27 %	C		2	D	58 %	B
	3	A	47 %	B		3	A	21 %	B
	4	A	35 %	D		4	C	34 %	D
	5	C	21 %	D		5	C	46 %	B
Test 7	1	A	35 %	B	Test 18	1	D	59 %	A
	2	B	78 %	C		2	B	30 %	D
	3	C	48 %	D		3	B	62 %	A
	4	D	59 %	A		4	B	74 %	D
	5	C	56 %	A		5	A	72 %	D
Test 8	1	B	69 %	D	Test 19	1	D	42 %	C
	2	C	75 %	D		2	B	40 %	D
	3	A	42 %	C		3	A	46 %	B
	4	C	33 %	A		4	B	79 %	C
	5	D	44 %	A		5	C	32 %	A
Test 9	1	C	40 %	A	Test 20	1	B	59 %	A
	2	D	62 %	A		2	C	60 %	B
	3	B	17 %	A		3	C	43 %	D
	4	C	42 %	A		4	B	38 %	A
	5	D	42 %	B		5	B	36 %	A
Test 10	1	A	49 %	B	Test 21	1	A	16 %	B
	2	A	42 %	B		2	C	49 %	A
	3	A	39 %	B		3	A	28 %	B
	4	C	21 %	A		4	B	32 %	D
	5	D	54 %	C		5	D	33 %	A
Test 11	1	D	70 %	C	Test 22	1	A	51 %	C
	2	C	39 %	D		2	D	77 %	B
	3	A	26 %	B		3	C	39 %	B
	4	A	77 %	B		4	D	53 %	B
	5	D	32 %	A		5	B	40 %	C
Test 12	1	B	46 %	C	Test 23	1	D	28 %	C
	2	A	83 %	B		2	C	34 %	D
	3	B	46 %	C		3	C	31 %	B
	4	D	76 %	A		4	A	37 %	B
	5	A	33 %	C		5	A	58 %	D

測驗	題號	正確選項	錯誤率	最多人選的錯誤選項
Test 24	1	C	46 %	A
	2	C	35 %	B
	3	B	52 %	A
	4	C	30 %	D
	5	A	46 %	B
	6	C	60 %	A
Test 25	1	D	63 %	C
	2	D	71 %	A
	3	B	55 %	C
	4	D	23 %	B
	5	D	39 %	C
	6	A	27 %	C
Test 26	1	C	42 %	A
	2	D	31 %	A
	3	A	40 %	D
	4	B	65 %	C
	5	B	69 %	D
Test 27	1	A	67 %	C
	2	D	36 %	A
	3	C	33 %	B
	4	C	75 %	A
	5	C	31 %	A
Test 28	1	A	26 %	D
	2	B	69 %	A
	3	D	36 %	B
	4	A	82 %	D
	5	A	88 %	D
Test 29	1	D	36 %	A
	2	B	29 %	C
	3	C	52 %	A
	4	D	24 %	B
	5	B	58 %	A
	6	C	49 %	A
	7	C	25 %	B
	8	C	19 %	A
	9	A	88 %	D
Test 30	1	B	68 %	C
	2	A	27 %	B
	3	C	63 %	A
	4	C	35 %	B
	5	A	52 %	B
Test 31	1	B	47 %	D
	2	B	42 %	A
	3	B	29 %	C
	4	D	32 %	A
	5	A	57 %	B
	6	D	63 %	A
	7	A	38 %	B
	8	A	22 %	C
	9	D	68 %	B
Test 32	1	D	24 %	A
	2	C	28 %	A
	3	D	31 %	A
	4	B	25 %	A
	5	A	20 %	B
	6	A	92 %	C
	7	B	55 %	D
	8	A	28 %	C
	9	A	55 %	B
	10	D	22 %	C
Test 33	1	C	36 %	B
	2	D	58 %	C
	3	A	40 %	B
	4	B	66 %	A
	5	D	52 %	B
	6	D	67 %	B
	7	D	47 %	A
	8	B	55 %	A
	9	B	79 %	C
	10	A	45 %	C
Test 34	1	C	33 %	A
	2	D	43 %	C
	3	B	48 %	A
	4	C	31 %	B
	5	A	50 %	B
Test 35	1	B	32 %	A
	2	B	74 %	C
	3	C	42 %	B
	4	A	44 %	D
	5	C	63 %	B
	6	C	36 %	A
	7	C	66 %	D
	8	B	41 %	A
	9	A	79 %	B
	10	D	81 %	A
Test 36	1	C	62 %	B
	2	A	19 %	D
	3	B	42 %	C
	4	C	70 %	B
	5	C	23 %	A
	6	D	53 %	B
	7	B	81 %	C
	8	B	60 %	C
	9	D	82 %	B
	10	C	68 %	B
Test 37	1	C	25 %	B
	2	A	44 %	C
	3	C	30 %	B
	4	C	55 %	D
	5	B	37 %	C
	6	A	52 %	B
	7	B	43 %	D
	8	A	63 %	C
	9	A	34 %	B
	10	D	20 %	C
Test 38	1	B	60 %	A
	2	C	30 %	B
	3	B	26 %	C
	4	D	57 %	B
	5	C	37 %	C
	6	B	86 %	A
	7	D	60 %	A
	8	D	60 %	A
	9	A	36 %	B
	10	C	57 %	A
Test 39	1	B	47 %	A
	2	A	61 %	B
	3	A	62 %	D
	4	C	38 %	B
	5	D	60 %	B
	6	D	41 %	B
	7	C	57 %	D
	8	A	50 %	C
	9	C	56 %	A
	10	A	50 %	A
Test 40	1	A	24 %	C
	2	D	47 %	C
	3	B	45 %	A
	4	C	46 %	B
	5	A	36 %	C